DON'T LOSE YOUR DESTINY

A Guidebook to Balanced Living

by Jim McCleary

First Edition

YES! ENTERTAINMENT
Minneapolis, MN

Don't Lose Your Destiny
A Guidebook to Balanced Living
By Jim McCleary

Published by:
YES! Entertainment
12866 Highway 55
Minneapolis, MN 55441

First printing 2000
Printed in the United States of America

Cover and text design by MacLean & Tuminelly
Cover illustration by Corbert Gauthier

Library of Congress Control Number 00-131593
ISBN 0-9679693-4-4

Notice
This is an information book. We do not claim to offer professional advice. If professional advice is expected, a professional with competence should be selected.

This book only covers a fraction of the material available on the subjects presented. Please seek further information from the references provided or other sources as necessary to meet your individual needs.

There may be mistakes in both content and typing in this book. The text should be viewed as simply a general guide. It is not the ultimate source of information on the topics covered. Much new information is discovered daily on these topics, and the reader should seek this information out.

This book was created to provide information and share the experience of a single person. Neither the author nor the publisher accept any responsibility or liability for any loss or damage suffered or alleged by any person who utilizes the information contained in this book.

You may return this book for a full refund to YES! Entertainment if you do not wish to agree with and be bound by the above.

Table of Contents

List of Charts and Maps

Introduction

I FELT COMPELLED to write this book in hope that by doing so I could help others avoid some of the pain and mistakes I have made in my life. After over a dozen years of successful business experience, I came to realize that something significant was still missing from my life, and that it was spiritual. It took me another twenty years to get to a modest level of understanding – and then only after many fits and starts, dead ends, and much frustration.

This book may help others understand how life's difficult situations can be explainable and fulfilling, rather than overwhelming and hopeless. Discovering these truths has brought me peace, assurance, and boldness in my many times of struggle.

I believe that the time is short, both for our lives and for the years that remain prior to cataclysmic times. However, few, if any, of our leaders understand this reality. I hope that this book will provide clarity to those interested in a practical understanding of these coming events but are unable to spend sufficient personal time in study due to other pressures. Our country surely has the best profile for supporting God's purposes on behalf of His people.

God's Plan For Today

Introduction to Part One

I BELIEVE THAT STORYTELLING is the best method for communicating meaningful information. The story I know best is the story of my life, with all of its high and low points. I thought that if I could use my life story to explain how I got into studying spiritual matters and how that gradual understanding has helped me, it might compel others to get more interested in understanding God's programs and their own spirituality.

Chapter 1

My Life, My Search

I WAS BORN in a small Midwestern farming community into a middle-class family just six months before my dad was to enter WWII. Because I didn't see much of him until I was through my formative years, my mom became my primary role model. She is a bright and industrious woman but, like many of us, carried certain childhood wounds into adulthood without the benefit of helpful and healing advice. I have learned with age that this should be no surprise, that solid advice for real healing is extremely difficult to find for any of us, even with the resources of our day and age.

As the eldest child I made the pacesetting steps for our family into a very different era. Although I possessed a lot of energy and drive, I didn't usually push the limits. In retrospect, I feel comfortable saying that I was pretty obedient, soft-spirited, and kind-hearted.

In school, my energy found its way into extracurricular activities, student government, and, to a lesser extent, sports. As I look back now, even though I was very successful even at that age, I developed low self-esteem early. I wasn't aware that I undervalued myself. People tell me that nowadays I come off as confident, but in those days I almost totally lacked confidence in spite of my performance and I therefore lacked a vision for what I might achieve in life.

To offset that handicap somewhat, I practiced diligence – just plain focused hard work. I always wanted to be the fastest and best at the things I did. I learned to enjoy leadership because I quickly discovered that I was not satisfied with the status quo or limited horizons. I was driven. I took on tough jobs to challenge myself and learn to overcome. I learned early to worship the god of performance and for much of my life have subconsciously oriented myself toward life situations where that god would engage. By doing so, I received the strokes that filled the void I was unaware of in my soul.

My public school class had just under one hundred members. I would guess that if a poll were taken of my former classmates and teachers today, the opinion would be that I was in leadership because of energy, drive, and willingness to undertake difficult tasks, rather than brilliance or charisma. I wasn't a member of the "in" crowd or the elite (such as it was in our small city). Most of my classmates would be surprised at the success I have achieved.

My spiritual life was classical small town for that time. Everyone went to church. It was expected. All the "nice" families did it. But it was dead. Stone dead. And hypocritical.

From my perspective that was dishonest, so I disliked, and eventually lost a fair amount of respect for, spiritual things. My dislike didn't extend to God, just to what I saw of many people practicing religion. Their hypocrisy made me angry. I went to church to conform, but when I saw church people routinely swearing, taking God's name in vain, and acting in ungodly ways hundreds of times a day, I came to think of it as powerless, empty, and phony. Since I prided myself on truthfulness, I didn't voluntarily spend time there. Besides, nothing confirming happened in our home.

I entered the military after high school for simple reasons. Because of my low self-esteem I did not perceive myself to be college material and I certainly didn't believe that I had the funding to see college through. Although I didn't acknowledge it, I then considered education beyond trade school to be unlikely. If I had thought about it clearly, classmates with lower performance levels than mine had entered college without a second thought. However, I didn't see it for myself. I was ready to leave home and military service was mandatory at that time, so I decided to get it out of the way.

I was not prepared for what I encountered. I was soon into smoking and drinking with most of the other enlisted men. The values I left home with soon dissipated under strong peer pressure. I had no moral gyroscope because I had no meaningful, solid spiritual foundation or role model.

After three years my enlistment was up and I returned home without a plan for the next step in my life. I was tougher, more cynical, more experienced, and totally divorced from anything spiritual. Not hateful, simply separated.

I didn't find suitable work in my small hometown, so I moved to the city to take a promising job in electronics service. I quickly found out that I could barely earn enough to support myself, let alone a future family. I soon knew that I needed to make some changes. A thoughtful and caring coworker whom I respected suggested I go to college. Soon a different job materialized, making that possible.

A little over four years later – and quite to my surprise – I emerged with a business degree. Because I was opportunistic, I entered the computer sales field. My career started off nicely and I moved from company to company several times to meet personal and professional objectives during the chaotic early years of that industry.

By 1979 I was the president and co-owner of a small computer distribution firm with a prenegotiated option to purchase the balance of the company. I thought I was on top of the world professionally but I still felt an unexplainable emptiness inside. The professional success, the recognition, the income and the toys didn't fill that void. I could already see that more hard work, more success, and further accomplishment wouldn't make any substantial difference to my inner self. More power, more money, more responsibility, and a bigger bank account wouldn't fill the vacuum inside my soul. I wondered, "Is this all there is to life?"

By that time I had also become even more cynical toward spiritual things because of the behavior I observed from so-called Christians. I had encountered several people who mentioned that they were Christians or wore an identifying lapel pin and, based on the numerous times I had been burned by their kind, found that they could almost always be distrusted. They often used guilt-inducing language to get at my pocketbook. I had no trust for any of them.

After going through a painful divorce, I decided to resume reading the Bible – a book that I respected but didn't understand. I bought a brand new copy thinking that would motivate me. A clerk in the bookstore advised me to get an everyday language version. I chose the Living Bible with Study Guide.

When I had tried reading the Bible several times earlier in my life, I had always begun with either the first book of the Old Testament or the first book of the New Testament. I consistently lost interest by the time I had read a few books. Then, once again, it went on the shelf to collect dust.

I made the same mistake this time and started with Matthew. The thought never occurred to me to start anywhere else. However, this time I was able to hang in there because the Bible was in everyday language. I discovered the book to the Romans. That's where I should have started in the first place! From God's perspective, the Romans represent the non-Hebrew people of our time who do not have a relationship with God. The book is all about God's "deal" for our times. Romans is for people like me who need a summary of God's programs to get started on this somewhat complex subject. The book of Romans (in modern language, not the King James version, in which Romans is almost indecipherable) started to turn my life around.

As I read further, I discovered the book of Hebrews, which is for the Jews of our time. For God's "chosen people," the blood-

Israelis, the book of Hebrews is the present-day counterpart to the gentile book of Romans. In it they will find the connections between the Mosaic "law" and the covenant applying to our post-Messiah time. Likewise, it is very useful to gentiles to better comprehend God's present point of view toward people of Hebrew descent.

Romans was not written to some group that I could not relate to, but to me and others like me with a similar background and experience set. My highly compartmentalized male brain could process this succinct twenty-page summary of God's program for our time. I read Romans over and over in the Living Bible. I studied it instead of simply reading it. It explained many things to me that I had had some basic understanding of, but could never quite fully put together.

Eventually, I moved on to Paul's other books and, with the background of Romans and the help of the study guide, began to enjoy and make sense of them for the first time. Many of the apparent inconsistencies of the Bible began to disappear. I soon found myself in a personalized search for God's truth directly from the word of God instead of a version that was twisted by some scholar from the 1500s or a present-day denominational interpretation. I complemented my reading of the Living Bible with the written and taped testimonies of other "open" and studious people. I began to dedicate fifteen to twenty minutes a day to the process and changed my drive-time radio to teaching tapes or contemporary religious music.

In a matter of a few months I decided to truly accept God, His Book, and His promises totally and *literally* in my life. Everything else in my life became subordinate to seeking, learning, and living what I found in the Bible. I began to trust my spiritual intuition about things. My already strong business ethics became even stronger. I began to tithe and offer with cheerfulness even when under financial stress and was regularly surprised by the results as I learned to wait for them.

As it turned out, it was a good thing that I got into study when I did and as deeply as I did; my life was soon to be severely tested. Just after exercising my option to purchase the company, disaster struck on three fronts almost simultaneously.

First of all, we found out that our second child, a daughter, was handicapped, that her life would be very difficult, and that she might not live long.

Second, our business bank, which had been our lender for many years, hired a new CEO who disliked high-technology leveraged-buyout customers. He gave us thirty days to find a replacement lender for our multi-million-dollar loan, which had never been in jeopardy.

And thirdly, the major product supplier to our business, representing over 70 percent of our volume, decided to drop us as they modified their distribution programs.

All of this meant certain family and financial disaster along with probable bankruptcy and career ruination for me.

Fortunately, by that time I was strong enough spiritually to endure the pain and wounds of these three simultaneous events. The most difficult one was observing our daughter in constant pain and the consequent suffering going on in our family.

Over the course of nearly twenty years I have come to understand, from the viewpoint of an ordinary man, the explanation for her suffering, the source of life's pain, and alternately the source of peace in our lives. The purpose of this book is to share those discoveries with anyone interested.

To be sure, God is good when we listen and patient when we don't. I became more balanced in my lifestyle, more secure and confident. I learned to trust my emotions as well as my intellect. Our daughter did go to Heaven early. Our company survived its onslaught. We eventually sold out to General Electric after becoming one of the very top systems integrators in our industry.

I ask forgiveness of those who would remind me of my early errors but I no longer permit those mistakes to affect my life. I simply put one foot in front of the other every day and try to do my best, realizing that I will encounter issues. However, I also have come to believe that all things will turn out right in the end, that the purposes for issues in life will be revealed, and that I will move on to my real home before I know it.[1]

My hope is that what I discovered in God's Word will provide encouragement and perhaps even hope and guidance to some of you during our challenging time on planet Earth.

May God bless and encourage you as you read this.

Notes, Chapter 1

1   Rom. 8:28, NL

Abbreviations

DK   Dake Bible, Dake Publishing, Lawrenceville, GA
NL   New Living Study Bible, Tyndale House Publishers,
      Wheaton, IL
NT   New Testament
OT   Old Testament

Chapter 2

Our Struggle

OR MANY OF US, once a modicum of money, maturity, and health have been secured, our focus becomes introspective. Questions such as "Why are we here?" and "What is life all about?" begin to arise once we have financial means and have knocked ourselves silly with fun and various forms of consumption.

Although these questions have confounded mankind for centuries, I believe that the answers are readily available, albeit somewhat hidden due to the distractions of life's momentum and our own passivity, unless we find ourselves in pain. Even then, true answers can be hard to find because we look for them in the wrong places. We seek completion from the material realm instead of realizing that only by acknowledging and dealing with the essential character of our basic natures, our spirits, can we achieve understanding. We search for relationship perfection with others as flawed and unable to fulfill us as we ourselves are instead of focusing on the essence of who we are. Satan plays a huge role in distracting and confusing us in this regard, as we will see.

To better understand what life is all about, it is helpful to contemplate our fundamental makeup. We have three major components: a body, a soul, and a spirit.[1] In our culture, we tend to bring intense personal focus to the first two, while assigning the care of the latter to others, if we consider it at all.

The body is a principal area of concentration. In most cases, we regularly live far in excess of the conditions required to meet our basic needs for food, clothing, and shelter. We would be amazed if we could calculate the percentage of our Gross National Product that is involved in meeting the *perceived* needs of our bodies. Advertising plays a large role here. We can read about the conditions of earlier generations to get perspective on the subject but most of us fail to realize how dominated our thinking is with meeting the wants of our bodies.

The soul is defined as the seat of our intellect, desires, feelings, passions, emotions, and appetites. It is the battleground for our will over issues of right and wrong. Here, once again, we are in overdose. It seems like there is an opportunity for every interest and appetite, and a plethora of emotional and intellectual guidance for almost any situation.

It is amazing. A few years ago prognosticators were suggesting that because our basic physical needs are being met primarily by machinery we would soon experience a labor glut. But nothing could be further from the truth. We are all working harder than ever and at an ever-increasing pace and level of stress. We have literal armies of consultants, counselors, and attorneys who, in theory, help us to understand and deal with life's ever-increasing complexities. The myth that mechanization would provide a lifestyle richer in overall content has been realized. Whatever efficiencies have been gained in production have been more than consumed by the needs of the hungry soul.

And finally, the spirit. We really don't do very much with the spirit, outside of "church," that is. Unfortunately, many of us have found that churches sometimes seem to do as much to harm the understanding of the spirit as good.

We will look at these three elements describing mankind more closely from the standpoint of God, as best we can understand it from His writing. He communicates His programs for us as individuals in His Book, the Bible. No particular religion, sect, or denomination's teaching will prevail in this discussion.

The Body

It is said that our body is designed to live three score plus ten, a bit more if we are lucky.[2] We get seventy years, more or less. After that we're on borrowed time.

While the body is a magnificent entity, we know empirically that our bodies will eventually die. What happens to our bodies after death?

I became very convinced of life after death after reading Dr. Raymond Moody's secular book *Life after Life*. Based on his observations of a large number of life-after-death incidents, Dr. Moody concludes that our spirits absolutely continue to exist after our bodies die.

But what happens to our body after death?

The Destiny of our Bodies

We are told in the Bible that our bodies, after death, will be res-urrected (rise again to life at a later time).[3] We should realize that, as with many things spiritual, the matter of human resurrection has long been a subject of considerable debate, even among the Hebrews (the curators of God's Word).

During the Roman era, the Hebrews were split into two major groups over this issue. The Sadducees did not believe in bodily resurrection at all, whereas the Pharisees did. And the Pharisees believed that only the bodies of "good" people live forever. They did not believe in a resurrection for the unjust, which is clearly taught in later Scripture.[4]

In fact, any study of spiritual matters will quickly lead to controversy. The only way I have found to sort these controversies out is to study and listen carefully to my intuition, keeping in mind that there is an evil side attempting to keep me from real truth.

The Bible clearly teaches not only that every body is resurrected, but that there are two separate, permanent resurrection events for our bodies, one for the good and one for the evil. These two resurrection events are to occur at different times in the future. Every human ever conceived will be resurrected. The first resurrection will be for those forgiven of their sins. The second, a thousand years later, will be for those who have not appropriated God's sole means of sin atonement.[5]

The Context of Time

As stated in the Bible, the "first" life of our body is brief, seventy years, more or less. In contrast to the length of our existence, which is forever, our first bodily life lasts only the equivalent of an instant. But it is during this "instant" (which, as we live it, can at times seem so unbearably long) that we choose the eternal destiny of our spirits and our resurrected bodies. We make this decision, usually only semiconsciously, by our behavioral choices. We are driven to seek understanding of these matters as we have the time, means, motivation, and energy. For most of us, some form of motivation is required. Sometimes that motivation comes as we experience pain or encounter circumstances that provoke us to ponder our near future. Without a sudden motivation, others tend to consider these issues later in life whether they have the time, means, and energy or not.

The Results of Our Choices

So "first" life is the period of time in which we choose between the only two options available for the eternal destiny of our bodies and spirits.

I used to believe that there was a third option: that when I died I would simply just disappear. I have since learned that there are only two options, not three. Just Heaven or Hell.[6] The mythical third alternative of simply fading away is not offered in God's Book. It is a trick of the evil side.

Hell is widely understood to be an awful place. I have read several books such as Dante's *Divine Comedy* and Thigpen's *Gehenna* that attempt to dramatize the conditions in Hell for our bodies and spirits. They are horrific! The Bible has a dramatic story about it, too.[7] Still, in our day-to-day lives we seldom take seriously the reality of Hell. If it were real to us, why wouldn't all of us get earnest about understanding these issues? The plain fact is that most of us feel too busy, have been too hurt by hypocrites claiming to have the answers, or are too distracted to put forth the effort necessary to understand our choices.

The risk we take in delaying the choice is that we cannot know how long we have to make that choice. None of us know with certainty how long we have here, and when it's over, it is *over* – there are no second chances.

Free Will

By simple observation we can all acknowledge that we are given free will so that we individually have personal and total control over our behavior and, therefore, our spiritual destinies.[8] As we confront the choices available to us in life, we can choose either the right path – to do God's will – or to follow our "natural" desires.[9]

Some of the "natural" desires that can send us in the wrong direction are:

- sexual misconduct
- occult practices
- rage, hatred, and temper
- envy and jealousy
- murder
- loving false teachings
- immoderation[10]

I was involved in some of these behaviors, as most of us have been at one time or another. The results of these behaviors are disastrous but we can recover from them if, before we die, we seek atonement through the only means offered by God.[11]

The Soul

Our souls house our intellects and our emotions, which are our passions, desires, feelings, and appetites.[12] The soul is the battle-field upon which life situations are resolved.

Intellect

Humanity has worked on the development of the intellect for thousands of years. We make a huge investment in our intellect starting with preschool, if not before. This is followed by elementary, secondary, trade, college and/or university training. Education is often associated with productivity, security, completeness, happiness, and most other measurements of success in life.

Emotions

Emotions are an area of living in which we are just moving toward a modest level of maturity. Emotions are complex and difficult to understand, especially for many men. Our investments and our mistakes in understanding emotions have been huge. The truly well-balanced psychologist, psychiatrist, or counselor is largely a dream, yet we have not learned to turn individually to the only perfect advisor, God, and receive His counsel in spite of how painful it might be to our notions. Regardless of the outcomes, we simply spend more and more on "professional" counselors, naively hoping for results that rarely materialize.

One of the things that I have learned is that the good life cannot be achieved without the balanced development of our emotional and intellectual natures. Intellect alone has historically proven insufficient in producing quality outcomes. To become truly healthy, the emotions as well as the intellect and a healthy spirit must be involved in the decision-making process.

Before receiving counseling, I lacked considerably in this area – a problem that probably originated in my childhood. Any man, however, can overcome this weakness through significant humility and purposeful study. For many men who struggle to understand emotions, balance is often arrived at by means of female assistance. Confidence and ability will come for most of us when we learn this balance of intellect and emotions.

Women, on the other hand, are more naturally comfortable with the balance. However, women sometimes overwhelm men with their emotional skill and tenacity, which can become intimidating to men. They can also sometimes permit emotions to override logic. In this case, the masculine character trait can bring the balance.

To become healthy, men must begin to develop and trust their emotional nature more and women must make allowances for this normal masculine deficiency. Men and women must be aware of these realities and accommodate them.

The Will

The will is the chooser. The will takes the input of the intellect, the emotions, and the spirit and processes a decision.

The will is a constant battleground for our intellect, emotions, and spirit. The outcome of these battles determines short-term behavior and, ultimately, the long-term destiny of our spirits at death and after resurrection.

We are choosing constantly. Many of the outcomes are consistent with God's desires for our behavior. But unfortunately, many things we do are displeasing to Him.[13] Depending upon the level of our sensitivity, we have a vivid awareness when our choices are wrong or right even as we make them. We also have a significant degree of control over them, depending upon our history, maturity, personal discipline, and any substance involvement.

God has written the rulebook but we are free to play our life game as we choose. He will not violate our right to free will. He will, however, allow circumstances to enter our lives that will motivate us to assess our wrong behavior. He will provide examples of better behavior. He will not give up on any of us regardless of what mistakes we make. At the end of the day, even if we repeatedly refuse to give up impure aspects of our lives, He will not force us to choose His way.

Morals

Morals involve distinguishing between right and wrong. A common belief in our time is that there is no absolute right or wrong, that as free-willed people we all have the absolute right to determine what is right or wrong for ourselves. The Bible states that God has established moral behavior limits that are acceptable to Him. I have personally found that ignoring those limits can lead to disaster.

The Conscience

We all come equipped with an internal moral gyroscope, the conscience, which confirms wrong behavior if and when we choose to listen.[14] (It doesn't work well for those hardened to listening to their inner voice.) We are not compelled by God to acknowledge or follow the prodding of our inner voice – that is left up to our individual free will.[15] Unfortunately, many of us allow our darker nature (which is also internal) to win the battle, resulting in long-term consequences that are always devastating.

Why were we "made" with these two conflicting personality aspects? Simply because God wanted to create beings like Himself, with the means and the opportunity to choose – correctly or otherwise. He did not want to create robots.

Sin

Sin is anything that is not in harmony with God's personality, standards, ways, and will. It exists in every single human.[16] That is not to say that everything we do is sin or that we all sin to the same degree but that we are all capable of sinning and that we do sin on a regular basis.

To be with God, however, there is a requirement that we be without sin, an impossibility for us, since we have a built-in bias to sin.[17] On the surface, it seems unreasonable that God should give us the capacity to sin while He alone has the right to determine acceptable behavior and to condemn us when we are unwilling to perform to those standards. At a minimum we would like to draw our own definitions of sin. Beyond that we like to convince ourselves that we sin only infrequently and, even then, only when influenced by another.

But God permits no easy excuses for our wrong behavior, except for being under the age of accountability or having reduced capability due to lack of mental ability or lack of information. God, who cannot abide sin, has graciously provided for those less capable. Neither children nor those with a reduced ability to understand are called to the same standard. Humans are expected to "walk" only to the level of their ability and revelation.[18]

We are not held to a standard about which we have no knowledge. However, the infidel who has not heard of the Bible is Hellbound if he has chosen to ignore the prompting of his conscience.

The tactic of intentional ignorance – that is, "winking" or hiding from the discovery of God's expectations to avoid being held to a higher level of accountability – doesn't work either. We are called upon to actively engage, to give time to these matters.

Fortunately, because we sin often, God has provided a way of making amends. But we must realize that we make this choice with our free will by means of our earthly behavior regarding sin.

The Spirit

Finally, we get to the spirit, that everlasting, never-dying part of us that is our connection to God or, if we so choose, the evil alternative. We know that the spirit is always awake during our first life. It is also permanently awake in either Heaven or Hell after we die.[19]

Least Understood

The spirit is the least understood of our three parts. One of the major reasons is that our scientific, proof-driven educational system has difficulty accepting things that are invisible. And our spirits, like God, are invisible.

Wholeness

To achieve wholeness, we *must* acknowledge our spirits because they are a part of us. This is not easy for a couple of reasons. First of all, spiritual matters take time to really comprehend and our time is already overbudgeted. If we invest anything at all in our spirits, we typically hire out the job of developing our individual spirits to professionals (i.e.clergymen). This doesn't work as well for our spiritual component as it does for our bodies and souls.

Secondly, we have serious defects in our spiritual teaching systems. Many of these teaching systems have grown to be based strongly on the "doctrines of men," rather than a straightforward reading of the subject matter.[20] In almost any other area of life, principles stated as clearly as they are in God's Word would be widely understood by now. But not so here.

Prideful positions taken by strong teachers in early times have sometimes led to an unhealthy division into various denominations that war and create division over minor issues. They struggle with each other over these minor doctrinal issues instead of addressing the real issues of mankind in a unified and godly manner.

In our times, some of our spiritual leaders have become overzealous or turn out to be hypocritical spiritually. Small wonder there is confusion. As a result, would-be participants in spiritual studies have been polluted during the battle in their wills. Because spiritual material is so deep, and because we have found it more natural and convenient to focus on body and soul, mining spiritual truths often takes a back seat. The exception is when we become desperate. Then, we often turn to God.

Since many of us only seek God when desperate, our spiritual muscles are weak. In fact, the majority of us are handicapped spiritually by our own laxity. Like it or not, overcoming these handicaps can be nearly impossible, but it can be done. God promises this to all, regardless of where they have come from or what mistakes they have made. All we are required to do is open the door of our hearts and He will come in.[21] However, the door only has a handle on the inside. He will not force Himself in. I know this to be true because I have been there myself and have learned that we must open the door ourselves.

We can become drawn into an understanding of spiritual matters after discovering that something is missing, something that can bring peace. This often comes after trauma or seeking peace by other means. For a few others, the connection seems to be naturally built-in – at least until serious stress strikes, and they then often find that they really don't have the answers.

The outcome is in each of our hands individually. The choice is ours. We can seek wholeness, balance, and peace in the worldly system presently under the control of Satan, or we can listen to our spirits and turn to God. In the familiar Lord's Prayer we are advised that God's will is presently not being done on earth: "Thy kingdom come and Thy will be done, on earth as it is in Heaven." In other words, His will is being done in Heaven now, but not yet on earth – and won't be until His kingdom arrives here. Yet we can have His will in our daily lives if we choose to. It's our choice to make. To receive it we must also receive His restrictions. If we are only willing to accept a God who is broad-minded and tolerant to our wishes, He is not for us.

Notes, Chapter 2

1　Thess. 5:23, NL
2　Pss. 90:10, NL
3　Dan. 12:2, NL; Jon. 5:28–9, NL
4　Mark 12:18, NL; Matt. 3:7, DK; John 5:28–9, DK; Rev. 19:11–15, DK
5　Rev. 20:6–11, NL
6　Dake Bible, OT page 620, col. 1–2 "Hell," OT page 622, col. 3 "Heaven"
7　Luke 16:19–31, DK
8　Deut. 30:19, NL; Rev. 22:17, NL
9　Gal. 5:19–21, NL
10　Dake Bible, note to Matt. 5:32; Lev. 19:26, 19:31, DK; Jas. 3:14, DK; Rom. 1:29, DK; James 3:16, DK; Num. 35:16–30, DK; Dake Bible, note to Acts 5:17; Phil. 4:5, DK
11　Deut. 30:19, NL
12　Dake Bible, NT page 226, col. 3 "Soul"

13　Pss. 14:3, NL; Rom. 3:10, NL
14　Rom. 2:12–15, NL
15　Mark 16:16, NL
16　Num. 15:30, DK; Jon. 1:29, DK; 2 Cor. 6:14, DK; Rom. 3:23, NL; 1 John 1:8, NL
17　Deut. 31:17–18, NL; Rom. 1:18–32, NL; Eccles. 7:20, NL; 1 John 1:8, NL
18　Jer. 31:33, DK; Dake Bible, notes to Rom. 2:12–15
19　Dake Bible, note to James 2:26
20　Matt. 15:8–9, NL
21　Rev. 3:20, NL

Abbreviations

DK　Dake Bible, Dake Publishing, Lawrenceville, GA
NL　New Living Study Bible, Tyndale House Publishers, Wheaton, IL
NT　New Testament
OT　Old Testament

Chapter 3

God's Viewpoint

T HE QUEST TO UNDERSTAND GOD and invite Him into our
lives begins for most of us with the most certain connection
He has provided for us, His Bible. The only way that we can
understand and interpret it is to read it carefully, slowly, and regularly. God has constructed His Book in such a way that it can
appeal to and be understood by persons of all backgrounds, religions, and intellects. Like everything else when dealing seriously
with God, His Book is like a custom-fit suit that changes shape
continuously as we develop. That is not to say that His policies
change, He just adjusts His presentation to fit our conditions, if
we listen. When we are diligent about studying it, regardless of
how often we read a section, something new will usually enter our
minds. As we consider what we are reading quietly, often that
something new will address some issue of the moment in our lives.

Understanding the Mystery of God

It is this particular mystery that is in view here. How can His Book
be written in such a way that it can provoke such a wide variety
of responses simultaneously? How can a dozen different people
studying together in the same room at the same time derive such
different meanings from the same verse or verses? It's the mystery of Scripture, and all genuine seekers experience the phe-
nomenon. It exemplifies the diversity and uniqueness of each

person, their individual situation, and God's individual and personal interest in each of us.

God in His wisdom constructed the Bible like a very intriguing puzzle, a puzzle that is not too difficult or too simple, that can be started anywhere in the Book, at any time, in any place, and that always produces consistent outcomes. His puzzle is one that can be picked up and put down. It challenges the most superior mind, yet can be understood by those less mentally gifted. It is a puzzle that we can best process in small, regular bites. The more one reaches into it, the more deeply one is drawn. The game is fun, the challenge of it unending. No one ever finishes. We are all called to it.

I found in my own life that once I decided to enter the process, it was easy to do. By disciplining myself to regularly give it a little time, I got into the habit and discovered that, overall, it is timesaving. By timesaving, I mean that all of us find that there is more to be done than we can usually expect to squeeze into a day without experiencing stress. I believe that this applies to almost everyone, at least, anyone that might be interested in this Book. I myself have experienced severe schedule-pressure as an executive and have observed it in all walks of life, as well.

When I get up a few minutes early and spend that time reading and meditating on a sentence or paragraph or two, or perhaps even a chapter, from the Bible, I have found that somehow everything gets done during the day and without stress (if I can remember not to self-induce it). Try it for thirty days and I believe that you will discover the magic of this reward.

As a result of this superior design, we are drawn into the study of understanding the mind of God, in whose image we are created.[1] And who doesn't want to understand their parent? It is by understanding Him that we can achieve peace.[2] It is by achieving peace that we can receive joy, make some sense out of painful and confusing situations, and get through life in a healthy and meaningful way.

God uses the puzzle design to help entice us to study His Word because he knows that understanding His Word will be necessary for us

- to hear from Him in new ways or on timely topics,
- to have enough knowledge so that we can distinguish false propositions from true doctrines of God,
- to avoid falling prey to Satan's wiles,
- to achieve success and wisdom.[3]

We are told to meditate on His instructions day and night.[4] But how can we do that without first getting enough true knowledge to have something to meditate on? The Bible has been constructed in such a captivating way that once we truly get started, momentum will keep us on track. As with many new but worthwhile things, getting started probably means thirty to forty forced repetitions. After that, it will become natural.

Other Mysteries of the Bible

For completeness we should acknowledge that there are other mysteries spoken of in Scripture. Significant among these (solvable) mysteries are the following:

- God, His kingdom, the universe, and eternity
- that gentiles as well as Hebrews are offered eternal life in Heaven
- the present blindness of Israel to His covenants and teaching
- God's master covenants
- the gospel
- the raptures
- the lawless spirit that exists among mankind
- faith

- God's use of Satan as a redemptive tool and His delay in eliminating him[5]

Darwin Versus Creationism

One of the most troubling issues that I had to deal with in accepting the Bible as a valid and accurate book for the rational mind was the question of the age of the earth. Here is what I found after study.

Taking the Bible as conventionally interpreted, our earth is about 6000 years old right now, with about 4000 of those years covered during the Old Testament period, which ended with the birth of Jesus of Nazareth, and 2000 years following. However, a careful study of portions of the Bible outside the first chapter of Genesis reveals biblical evidence that the earth had earlier life forms that existed prior to Genesis 1:3, which would be consistent with scientific findings.[6]

As it turns out, a very early flood is reported in the Bible that destroyed the creation that Satan was originally allowed to rule.[7] This destruction was necessary due to the extremely evil behavior of its inhabitants and their ruler, Satan (also called Lucifer). Satan's flood, reported in Genesis 1:2, fossilized these early life forms, which science now carbon-dates with the seemingly conflicting scientific conclusion that the earth is millions of years old.

As I read many commentaries on these matters carefully, I came to agree with the conclusion that this earlier creation (which preceded Adam's) existed during a *huge* interval of time between Genesis 1:1 and 1:2.[8] During that period, that is, after the original creation events of 1:1 and before the re-creation events of 1:3, millions of years passed.

Unfortunately, we customarily read these verses without understanding this time interval. We assume that, because the verses are next to each other without any warning about the interval between them, Genesis 1:1–3 are talking about the same time period. This is likely not the case.

I discovered that the fourth word in Genesis 1:2, "was," (Hebrew hayah), should be translated "became" or "came to pass" as it is 67 other times in Scripture.[9] Thus the phrase should be read as "And the world became without form and void." If the earth *became* empty, it obviously was previously not empty. This correction starts to get things on track. This position is further supported by other Scriptures such as Genesis 1:28, where Adam is told to replenish the earth, not to fill it for the first time.

After the re-creation described in Genesis 1:3 and beyond, Satan again came into power with the fall of Adam and Eve in accordance with God's covenant conditions.[10]

With this background, biblical integrity is maintained in harmony with scientific discovery.

The fallacy of evolution is very effectively argued in materials outside our scope. Suffice it to say that qualified scientists with open minds state that the probability of a single-celled organism developing into a creature over billions of years is the statistical equivalent of a tornado blowing through a junkyard and creating a rocket ship capable of reaching outer space safely. Not very convincing to me, either rationally or instinctively.

Harmony in Scripture

Another area that brought understanding and belief to me was the resolution of what appear to be disagreements on the same subject between various parts of the Bible. Also, there can appear to be disputes between what we interpret the Bible to say and what we observe to be facts. When these incidents occur, the integrity of the entire work can be put into question. One reader can choose to change or ignore one part of the Bible to accommodate his or her experience or beliefs and another reader can do the same to another section. Soon, nothing is firm. The result is chaos.

These conditions can threaten to destroy the overall credibility of the Bible and must be resolved. If not, the consequence will be severe damage to the acceptance and the effectiveness of the Scripture.

The Bible tells us that Scripture is "God breathed," or that "all Scripture is inspired by God."[11] Said another way, each original word in the original language was carefully chosen by the Divine. When inconsistencies seem to appear, we need to dig deeply to discover the real truth. Our attitude should be to inquire into the apparent inconsistencies with the intent of discovering interpretive errors rather than Divine errors. Given several scriptural texts on a subject, the majority generally rules. This does not mean that we should ignore what appear to be inconsistencies. Further study will generally lead to a correct understanding. With this attitude, and sufficient effort, harmony will triumph.

Resolving Apparent Inconsistencies in Scripture

Perhaps the best way to bring resolution to this matter is to illustrate how incorrect conclusions can be drawn. This may enable other potential discrepancies to be similarly processed on one's own. A majority of the supposed inconsistencies arise from only a few sources.

Misattribution

Misattribution happens most often when we assume that a biblical statement is the "inspired" theology of God, when it is simply the reporting of a biblical character's conversation or an historical incident.

In Job 1:21 we find the statement: "The Lord gave, the Lord taketh away, blessed be the name of the Lord." This statement is often attributed to God, and is usually taken as divine doctrine by theological leaders and laymen alike as they offer it up in explanation of a situation they can't rationalize in any other way. This initiates a false school of thought that God is an unpredictable divine being who arbitrarily causes people hurt. In reality, nothing could be farther from the truth. The strongest indicator that this conclusion is inconsistent is that Scripture elsewhere defines God's humane and caring personality and makes clear that He is a *personal* God who cares for each of us individually.[12]

The truth is that this verse merely reports a statement made by a man, Job, at a depressed moment in his life. It does not report God's doctrine. This misinterpretation has led to great pain and misunderstanding about God's character among the believer/seeker community.

Understanding the Audience

It is important to understand the intended audience when a statement is given. For example, is the audience Hebrew, gentile, or the church?

Huge errors can be made otherwise. One easily understood example is the application of all of the Law of Moses doctrines to members of the present-day church. These doctrines are separate and somewhat different, and are for different covenant periods. (See pages 83–86.)

Errors of Context

The propensity to become confused when not understanding the historical or cultural background of an event is illustrated when reading the following statement from Matthew 19 and Mark 10: "It is easier for a camel to go through the eye of a needle, than for a rich man to enter into the kingdom of heaven." Taking this literally, and with no further information, one would conclude that it is impossible to be simultaneously wealthy and godly. Out of this comes the myth that only the poor can go to Heaven. Does this really make sense? How can God get His programs to work on earth without money? It certainly caused me to hesitate as my business ventures became more successful.

Another reason this seems inconsistent is that we know that the disciples were primarily a collection of self-employed men and a government official. They were not poor.

When we understand that the "eye of a needle" was simply the name of the small gate used in walled cities after the main gates were closed for the evening, we achieve clarity. Camels got through the eye by being unloaded and crawling through on their knees.

Figurative Interpretations

A common error is assuming that biblical stories are figurative rather than literal, just nice little mythical tales. The truth is that all are to be taken literally unless it is contextually impossible to do so. They all contain messages about covenant doctrine, life choices, behavior, and theology. There are many examples in both testaments, but one that is commonly considered mythical is the story about Lazarus.[13] This story tells the truth about conditions in Hell. It also describes the now-empty compartment in Hell called Paradise, along with other features of Hell's landscape. The Messiah took the spirits of the righteous occupants of Paradise back to Heaven with Him after His planned death on earth following His first advent.

The confusion here, and in other stories that seem too bizarre to be real such as the crossing of the Red Sea and Jonah in the whale, is to conclude that they are simply cute little stories and don't report reality. However, recent research has established the plausibility of both of these tales.

Translation Errors

Translation problems from the original text occur frequently. Although much less a problem today as a result of newer translations, "workmen seeking to rightly divide the word of truth" must still occasionally seek to find the human error of the translators.[14] An example would be the Genesis 1:2 problem regarding the word "was" and "became" discussed previously. (See page 33.)

Almost all presently available versions of the Bible are worthwhile. I happen to like the New Living Version in part because it was the version that impacted my life the most initially and got me on the correct path. However, the NIV and others are fine too. I do want to make the very important point, however, that the most common version, the King James, should be avoided initially, *especially* for the all-important book of Romans. Romans is very confusing in the King James Version.

I like the Dake King James Version because it has the best and most concise study notes I have found, either adjacent to the text, or in an entirely separate commentary.

However, I believe that Dake, as well as other publishers, have arrived at some incorrect conclusions, as you will discover in later chapters. The reader should be prepared to be confused by the different conclusions drawn by the various sources, but should draw his or her own conclusions.

Misunderstanding God's Plan

When we do not have an overall, bird's-eye perspective of God's plan and programs from His point of view, it is easy to be confused. He shares His plans with us in His Book and, when we comprehend them, we are much better equipped to be aware of and defeat the programs of darkness. Without that viewpoint, we can easily miss the real situation. The understanding of God's overall programs is a special topic that I cover in part two of this book.

Accepting Inconsistency

A good example of how observed facts coupled with incorrect interpretations can result in a discounting of the rationality of the Scripture is the apparent inconsistency between the dating of the earth by fossil life studies and the misinterpretation of earth's age from Genesis. The problem with simply accepting what appear to be inconsistencies is that it subtly undermines the creditability of text. A better practice is to search out all instances that appear to contribute to the problem. Then, using a Bible with good study notes, process a conclusion by working through each of these areas from which apparent inconsistencies arise. When we search diligently enough, the creditability is always maintained and we learn interesting things in the process of clearing up confusion.

In conclusion, I have found that all Scripture harmonizes when all of the facts are on the table. When dealing with a questionable passage, put it through the filters discussed here, and the difficulty will usually disappear. When this is done, the Bible achieves its rightful status as a totally valid document from God that provides a firm basis upon which we can absolutely rely for life decisions. The Bible does not contradict itself, but it occasionally takes time and effort to understand why it may seem to do so.

Notes, Chapter 3

1   Dake Bible, ot page 618, col. 4 "Man's Creation" (3)

2   Prov. 3:1–2, nl; Jon. 14:27, nl

3   Dake Bible, nt page 157, col. 2 "Eight Ways God Speaks"; 1 John 4:1, nl; Eph. 4:18, nl; Dake Bible ot page 667, col. 3 "32 Facts"

4   Dake Bible, note to Phil. 4:8

5   Dake Bible, ot pages 53–4, col. 3 "30-fold Plan"; Eph. 3:2–7, 6:19, nl; Rom. 11:25, nl; I Thess. 4:15–17, nl; 2 Thess. 2:7, dk; 2 Cor. 4:18, dk; Heb. 11:1, dk; 2 Cor. 2:5–11, nl

6   Dake Bible, ot page 51, col. 4 "15 Things the Bible Does Not Say"

7   2 Pet. 3:5–7, dk

8   Dake Bible, ot page 53, col. 2 "Age of the Earth"

9   Dake Bible, note to Gen. 1:2

10 Gen. 1:3, dk

11 2 Tim. 3:16, nl

12 Num. 14:18, nl

13 Luke 16:22, dk

14 Beirle, Donald. *Surprised by Faith.* (1992)

Abbreviations

dk   Dake Bible, Dake Publishing, Lawrenceville, ga

nl   New Living Study Bible, Tyndale House Publishers, Wheaton, il

nt   New Testament

ot   Old Testament

Chapter 4

Confusing Concepts

A S I BECAME A SELF-TAUGHT STUDENT of the Bible, I
encountered with considerable interest answers to quite a
few matters that had confused me or contributed to my
indifference toward spiritual matters over the years. Understanding these matters has been very helpful to me in coming
into a close relationship with God and may be of some interest
to you as well. At the end of the day, I have found that God is
rational to me when I'm not confused and further, that when I
get a "check in the spirit" about something, I should listen up
because He is trying to provide me with an alert. Refining and
learning to trust my recognition of and response to this "check"
is now a major area of focus for me.

Anger

Anger is an emotion all of us have, including God.[1] Since God has
the emotion, we know that anger can serve a worthwhile purpose.

The problem with anger is that we often don't manage it properly and let it run out of control. This is generally worse than the
other end of the spectrum, which is to dishonestly attempt to
hide our anger or, equally unhealthy, attempt to bury it.

Our emotions, including anger, are given to us for many purposes. Among these is to warn us when something may be wrong.
Sometimes the issue that we perceive as wrong through our anger
trigger is merely a response to one of our own personal weak-

nesses rather than something that is really wrong. It takes maturity, much counsel, and a humble spirit to make that discernment.

For anger to be helpful rather than a liability, it must be properly harnessed. We must constantly be on guard when we feel our anger rising. Anger is misused most often because we don't properly control it.

We see in Ephesians the admonitions not to sin when we are angry and to work through our wrath, or rage, before the day's end.[2] Taking these two separately, we are permitted righteous anger in the case of a meaningful just cause, but we must not allow Satan to provoke us to unrighteous behavior as a result of the anger. Incidents of discourteous driving, for example, are not a just cause for anger. Drivers will make mistakes, be too aggressive, and occasionally even be unkind. We all do it from time to time, but we need to counsel ourselves to charitably dismiss these acts.

Uninvited sexual advances toward our children, on the other hand, are an example of a valid basis for anger. A good way to discern between the two is to examine whether or not the incident directly violates one of God's specific admonitions.

Working through our wrath before day's end means that those who choose to follow God's ways are, as individuals and not dependant upon other parties involved in the conflict, to discipline themselves to get over the flash of intense anger before the end of the day. They need to recognize that the behavior of the other party(ies) involved is outside their control and that their principle obligation is to get their own anger under control. It does not mean that if one gets into an argument with another at the end of the day, it is necessary to stay up all night to work out a complete and perfect resolution, especially if the other person has not managed his anger. It does not mean that a perfect solution must be in place. The result of holding out for a perfect solution may simply be a meaningless cave-in by one of the parties in order to get to sleep.

Backsliding

The story of Balaam as presented in the Old Testament is a primary lesson for understanding the loss of salvation.[3] Balaam was the son of the king of Edom, which is in present-day southwestern Jordan. He was an insincere follower of God who as an adult settled in Mesopotamia (present-day Iraq). He had a widespread reputation for having the gift from God of predicting the future and also the ability to pronounce curses or blessings on people. He was called on by the king of Moab, a small adjacent nation, to get God to curse Israel in exchange for a fee.

At first he was able to resist his appetite for the proffered rewards. But, even after knowing that God did not approve of the King's request, Balaam kept going back to Him to try to change His mind. Balaam practiced false belief and was not an honorable servant of God. He did not want God's will, he wanted his own. Moreover, he apparently thought his desires for the rewards were somehow secret from God.

God, recognizing that he would eventually rebel and go anyway, gave Balaam permission with the restriction that he could only go if the king of Moab's men came to get him and further, that he could speak only as God permitted. Balaam was also told to bless, instead of curse, Israel.

Predictably, Balaam was anxious for the riches and honor and left right away, before the King's men came to make another request for him to visit. This act of disobedience grated against God. God supernaturally interrupted Balaam's trip and Balaam then agreed to honor God's request to say only what He permitted.

Upon arrival, Balaam sacrificed properly, indicating his understanding of God's requirements and probably hoping for favorable position with God in the upcoming financial opportunity. Balaam obediently fulfilled his promises to God for awhile, but soon taught the Moabites how to trick Israel into sexual sin so that they would draw God's curse. That way, Balaam thought he would appear not to have a direct hand in causing the sin. In other words, Balaam was so anxious to get the Moabite money, he was willing to sabotage the innocent and disobey God. He was selfish. As we might expect, this did not please God.

Balaam was originally on the right path, and therefore blessed of God, but his true inner self was so desirous of riches and honor that he quickly gave up on the correct path in exchange for financial reward. Ultimately, he could be – and was – bought. He didn't have true, honest loyalty toward God and the corresponding conviction to flee from the temptation. He loved money and the honor of man above obedience. He willingly mixed with the ungodly. He learned to use religion for gain.[4]

Balaam returned home after teaching the Moabites. Once he had crossed over the line, things quickly got much worse for him. He soon got into witchcraft, probably because he lost his position of favor with God and hence his special powers. He became what the Bible calls a backslider: one who once knew God but came to reject Him. He ended his life as an enemy of Israel fighting for another nation against God's people.

The stories of many of today's hypocrites may not be quite so readily understood. They often act persuasively sweet and proper, but are skilled at deception so that even the most discerning can be confused. These people, to the inexperienced or the trusting, seem to know God. They pray. They will be obedient enough to His life-walk expectations to confuse others and cause them to believe that they are true persons of God. They obey God, sometimes. They resist worldly pressures, but only inconsistently. They stretch God's rules continuously. They keep one foot in the camp of God while their hearts are elsewhere.

One of Satan's principal program tools in dealing with civilizations today is trickery such as he used on Balaam, as we will see.

Apostasy

In order to complete the message of the story of Balaam, we must have a working understanding of this matter of backsliding, or apostasy. Counterfeit religious people come from several sources, including

- those who intentionally, and from the start, misuse the church or God's name for their own benefit rather than in service to His purposes (the minority),
- those who once knew Him but, like Balaam, fell away,
- those who know a little about God from one source, but fall under the influence of Satan through pride or some other dysfunction.

To teach us how to identify these phonies by their conduct, God has provided lists of behaviors in the Bible that indicate those who falsely practice godliness. We need to be strong in trusting our intuition and our inner voices so that we recognize these behaviors in others and overcome their effect in our lives. We should understand how these people can bring confusion, wariness, anger, and distrust toward things spiritual and must discount them if we desire to be healthy.

The first list is found in Romans. Here God identifies characteristics fitting these people.[5] Only one of these behaviors, strongly practiced, is necessary for a person claiming to be godly to be classified as a backslider:

- vices contrary to justice and right living
- sexual sins
- wickedness and depravity
- vicious disposition and desires
- envy at the sight of another's good fortune
- murder or hate of another
- causing strife and discord

- lying, especially when done with guile, enticement, and subtlety
- putting the worst construct on every action
- secret detraction
- slandering or falsely accusing the absent
- hating sacred things
- scorn, hate, and insolence
- pride
- self-exultation and vanity
- inventing evil things
- disobedience to (good) parents
- destitute of interest in spiritual things
- breaking covenants
- being without natural affection
- unforgiving spirit of noncompromise
- pitiless and cruel

From 2 Timothy we have another list.[6] Again, one or more symptoms from this list indicate hypocrisy (you will notice some duplications):

- self-love (narcissism)
- covetous (inordinately desiring what belongs to another)
- boastful (braggarts)
- prideful
- blasphemous (contempt or lack of reverence for God)
- disobedient to parents
- unthankful
- unholy
- without natural affection
- truce-breaking
- falsely accusing
- without moral restraint
- fierce (violently hostile or aggressive in temperament)

- despising those who are honestly good
- traitorous
- rash
- high-minded (senseless, conceited)
- loving pleasure to an immoderate level (overly sensual)
- always learning but never coming up with the truth
- resisting truth

In order to distinguish hypocrites, the Bible advises us to be "wise as serpents, and harmless as doves," to discern others by their fruit (the results arising from their actions), and to ignore their words while watching their behaviors.[7]

God also tells us that many will say "Lord, Lord," and He won't know them because the "fruits" of their lives confirm their ungodliness, their true hypocritical nature.[8] Don't worry, God is not fooled, ever.

Let's not allow our anger over these kinds of people to steal our future or hurt our present-day lives.

Born Again

Early in my walk with God I found the term "born again" to be very confusing.

Being born again simply means receiving and acknowledging a new birth of our spirits. We shift from the normal state of largely ignoring spiritual matters or being altogether turned off, to becoming active in our seeking of the true spirituality of God.[9] There is no magic here, no formula, no certain place or denomination. Anyone can do this, and it may even be most easily done in private study.

There is generally not a great emotional event associated with becoming born again. Being born again is simply the result of a process of learning to understand God. It usually doesn't happen right away, but it doesn't take long, either – if we are serious.

To become open to receiving the truth, many of us need to leave behind our cultural religions as well as the hurts and distrust arising from previous experiences with supposedly spiritual people or groups. This is difficult. Everyone can do it, but not many do.

God will let us fall into trials in life so that we will feel pressure to seek, but it is easy to be pulled off course.[10] He will even let those already grounded in understanding suffer as an example to others, so that they will seek.[11]

Indications that this process is underway in someone will be a change in heart, motives, desires, will, life, and conduct. This will be progressive. We can fall off the path, making it necessary to start the process over again.[12] The born-again status is not a stagnant state and should be maintained by continuous development.

A born-again person is really an altogether new person, a new creation, able to leave behind previous life mistakes and start all over with a clean slate.[13]

Communion

The sacrament of communion is a memorial practice that believers observe in recognition of the sacrifice of the Messiah.[14] The wine or fruit juice represents His sin-atoning blood. His sinless blood constitutes the only covenant-provided mechanism with the power to absolve people from their sins and thereby make them acceptable to God.[15] (See page 99.) Sins must be absolved for each of us before entry into Heaven is permitted.

The believers of old, prior to the first coming of the Messiah, transferred their sins onto the head of a perfect substituting animal.[16] The animal was interim provision prior to the arrival of the perfect being, the Messiah, whose sacrificial death atoned for all past, present, and future sins for those who believe in Him.

The bread represents the body of the Messiah. His perfect and sinless body is the substitute for our sinful bodies. We can now transfer our sins onto His body by faith.[17] The transfer of our sins onto the Messiah, who is the perfect substitute, enables us as sinners to have our record of sin wiped clean and to enter Heaven.

The practice of substituting animal sacrifice for the absolution of sins is no longer necessary since the Messiah has fulfilled His duties.[18] This practice, however, will be reinstituted by the Hebrews on Temple Mount in Jerusalem during the upcoming period of tribulation.[19]

Communion is a straightforward concept that has unfortunately been corrupted by many organizations that put conditions on observance. Communion can be practiced at any time and as often as desired, presuming it is done by believers and in the right spirit. Any other limitations are the construct of man and without scriptural support.

Evil Spirits

Satan has a huge army of evil spirits, or devils. They each seem to be very singular in skill and purpose, and it seems that they need to occupy a human or animal body in order to operate in the material world.[20]

Evil spirits serve Satan by causing sickness, torment, lying, violence, lust, false doctrines, and every imaginable kind of evil. They can be powerful, fierce, wrathful, and conversely friendly when it suits their purpose. Thousands of them can enter into one person at the same time. All unbelievers are somewhat in common purpose with them.[21]

They are subject to the Messiah, however, and can be discerned, resisted, and cast out by believers, although to do so requires knowledge and significant effort. Evil spirits will end up in Hell at the end of the upcoming millennium of divine government.[22]

Diligence

Success, defined as the attainment of worldly wealth, favor, or eminence, does not require godliness, but it usually requires diligence. God often permits the rewarding of diligence whether the person is following Him or not.[23]

That is not to say that all of those successful in the worldly sense are diligent. There are other ways to success, such as inheritance, luck, and rewards from the dark side. These are usually temporary, and they rarely contain the "riches without sorrows" promised by the Bible.[24]

Because we equate present-day prosperity with eternal success, it is sometimes surprising or confusing to the believer that God permits the rewarding of the ungodly with worldly success.[25] We need to recognize that the two are not connected. (Not are all of the diligent are successful, at least not in worldly terms.) God works in mysterious ways and we need to trust Him.

Dual Coming of the Messiah

Another misunderstanding, especially for the Hebrews, is the dual coming of the Messiah. The Hebrews expect only one coming of Him, as King. His first coming, as a suffering servant, was understood by only a few. The Old Testament predicts the coming of the Messiah over 100 times, including many predictions requiring two comings.[26] This has provided much confusion, argument, and misfortune over the years.

Eternal Security

There is a concept that once people have secured eternal life in Heaven by their earthly choices they can never lose it, regardless of what they do or how ungodly their lives on earth later become. Some believe that earthly baptism accomplishes this end. This theory of "once saved, always saved" is commonly referred to as eternal security.

In the event that a person who we think is Heaven-bound begins conducting his life in an ungodly way, the popular explanation is that the person was not truly saved anyway.

This entire line of thinking is very uncomfortable to me. It implies that we have the ability to judge the spiritual status of another. We don't. Only God knows for sure whether a person has made a real heart change. I believe that people can make a passionate decision about something and then fail to stick with that decision. (See the earlier sections on backsliding and apostasy.)

This is the reason the Bible is replete with information about the consequences of apostasy.[27] Check out the stories of Saul, Judas, Balaam, Ananias and Sapphira, and others to confirm these matters.[28]

Also, carried to the extreme, a variant of this line of thought holds that if a saved person fails to repent of *any* sin just prior to their physical death, they will go to Hell. That is, even though their heart has really been changed, God will cause the saved person to lose eternity over a minor technicality. This is certainly not a logical conclusion, either.

Guilt

We can feel unworthy or experience self-reproach because of previous or recent behaviors that we know are wrong and our inability to control them. Paul mentions this as his major struggle.[29] It is easy for us to become disgusted, angry, and frustrated with ourselves and just give up. We must recognize this as one of the major tools that the dark side uses to keep us separated from God.

God tells us that we are all sinners.[30] God has promised us that He is no "respecter of persons."[31] He tells us that no one, regardless of color, sex, intellect, experience, or any other factor, is any less susceptible or has any advantage over any other person when it comes to overcoming obstacles so we can be one with Him.

We need to own that truth. We are *all* worthy, regardless of what we have done or what has happened in our lives. We need to choose to concentrate on learning about Him and then do our best. He will always provide a way of escape from evil situations that is within our power if we are sincerely seeking Him.[32] We must not permit Satan to steal our hope and place us in bondage. If we do, we may become angry with God as we reflect on our behavior.

Holy Spirit

God's leadership team is made up of three entities, the Father, the Son (the Messiah), and the Holy Spirit.[33] Only one of these three, the Holy Spirit, is with us on earth here and now. His ministry is the pledge, or "earnest-money," for the promises made by God to the believer.[34] The Holy Spirit was sent to comfort, bring peace, teach, bring power to, intercede for, cleanse, guide to truth, and dwell in believers until the plan of God for our time is complete.[35]

Hypocrisy

One of the most interesting personalities to surface in American politics recently is Jesse Ventura, the ex-professional wrestler who in 1999 began serving his first gubernatorial term in Minnesota. Jesse got elected on the basis of his apparent honesty and bravado, his nonpolitical nature, and his in-your-face straightforwardness. He is a nonpolitical politician.

Among the many topics that Jesse, on his new platform, feels compelled to comment about is religion. He finds little value in the organized religion he has experienced in his life, a position that might resemble the average person's view. On the other hand, Terry, his wife, does believe religion is important.

Why is that? Was Jesse born with an adversity to religion? Is it in his genes? Did he exit the womb that way?

No. This is learned behavior. Somewhere along the way he got hurt or insulted by church people so he did what most of us do: he wrote off the whole experience and all people associated with religion, so far permanently. His experiences with judgmental, self-righteous, pseudo-religious phonies raise the hair on the back of his neck (what little there is) and really make him angry. Curiously, words or behavior inconsistent with what our natural instincts tell us about real godly behavior can upset all of us in a way that few things do. Most of us intuitively react the same way that he does.

The hypocrites that Jesse encountered are little, if at all, different from those of days long ago. They are often smug, closed to things outside or different from their own little worlds, critical of most things not familiar, and highly adept at concealing dysfunction by making others feel guilt, inferiority, stupidity, or discomfort. Voila! Here you have the stereotype of some church-goers as seen by the unchurched.

The error here is not in Jesse's feelings. His feelings most likely accurately reflect the treatment he observed. Being a perceptive person, he could tell their true feelings toward him by the communication of their eyes, regardless of their words. He is also bold and doesn't mind letting the public know of the results of his experiences – with religion or otherwise.

However, he has made an error. To use an old expression, he has thrown out the baby with the bathwater.

To give Jesse the benefit of doubt (and because there's just too much good about Jesse for me to believe otherwise), deep in his inner self he certainly must have consideration for humanity's cosmic struggle between God and evil. But because of his hurt (complicated by his busyness), his emotions prevent him from an honest intellectual pursuit of the subject.

We all accept rather easily the proposition that if God's people act like "that," we do not want to have a relationship with them or Him. Implicit in that choice are the assumptions that God has absolute control over the behavior and mindsets of the people who call themselves godly and that He uses His divine powers to prevent those who come in His name to be short of perfect.

On reflection, are these assumptions realistic? Well, no. Because we know that God has given us free will and with it, the ability to confuse and confound, or to be confused and confounded by, real truth.[36]

However, we typically don't think about religion much after an experience like Jesse's. What for? We can live without it, right?

The answer is that we cannot. Not if we want to experience real peace and joy in our lives. Because we all have the concept of God built naturally into us.[37] It may be hidden under a lot of rubbish heaped on us by people like those Jesse encountered, but it is still there. Most of us have ample opportunity in life to develop a hard protective shell against those incidents and the people and system they represent. This interferes with our natural appetite for understanding God.

After considering these things rationally, it is clear that people most often turn off to God because they are

- hurt by people who call themselves godly and develop a shell,
- taken up with the things of this world and don't think about it,
- raised in an anti-God or anti-Bible environment,
- simply confused.[38]

I had those some of those feelings and perhaps you do, too. Don't give up and lose your destiny. Fight back by studying and you will be richly rewarded.

Occult

God labels occult practices high sin. They are from Satan. Run, don't walk, from the following occult practices:

- Ouija boards
- superstitiously seeking guidance through witches (female), wizards (male), palm and tarot card readers, fortune-tellers, or other mediums
- superstitions such as lucky and unlucky days, signs, and omens in the skies
- attempts at supernatural communication with the dead, the evil, and others
- casting spells
- astrology, horoscopes, and star gazing[39]

These things are not simply harmless fun. They invite the wrong spiritual side in. These practices have thousands of years of harmful history.

Predestination

We sometimes hear or receive subtle teaching that God has pre-chosen certain individuals to achieve heavenly life, often referred to as predestination, election, or foreknowledge. This preselection is said to have happened regardless of the behavior choices (i.e. free will) of the people in question. God supposedly chose them ahead of time, rather than giving them the responsibility of selecting their own destiny by way of their own life choices.

In order to accommodate this teaching, one must conclude that the biblical teaching regarding free will is a farce, that there is really nothing we can do by our own choices to respond to God's prompting in our consciences and achieve (not earn, but achieve) Heaven, and that the battle for our spirits is all over before it begins.

This is what the Bible calls a "doctrine of man," that is, not a doctrine originated by God, but one developed here.[40] Many have been – and are presently – unwittingly taken in by these doctrines. In this case, it makes a falsehood of the principal programs offered by God, because if we cannot affect our eternal destiny by our behavior, why not simply live for the moment, do whatever feels good, live riotously? Behavior choices won't make any difference in the end, anyway, right?

But this is not what the Bible teaches. It teaches working toward one's salvation by choice, every day.

God has predestined *everyone* for Heaven, conditionally.[41] The condition is that we accept His programs and live them to the best of our ability within the understanding that we have.[42] We don't have to live them perfectly, only as well as we are truly able within the light provided. But if we reject them, He cannot do more.[43] His offer is firm: before the death of our bodies we must make the choice to live our lives to the best of our abilities according to our revelation of His expectations, or we will be lost.

God has foreordained all to come to Him, but many don't.[44] Being omniscient, He knows in advance who will make the correct choices. But the result is up to our own election, or choice. This plan is the same for all regardless of race, color, financial status, or any other distinction.

Strength

Many are confused when encountering someone known to be a believer who has a strong, rather than a malleable, character. We are conditioned to believe that believers should be soft. In fact, believers often discount the spirituality of another believer who is strong. Why is this? Our Messiah is strong and we are instructed to follow His example. Isn't this simply another way that believers are kept in line by the other side?[45]

That said, strength can also be an outward camouflage for inward weakness or power-seeking. Discernment is required. Counterfeiting is one of the most polished skills of Satan and his clan.

Wise, bold, strong believers are necessary to keep the believer community on track and productive. The spiritual and performance weaknesses of many of our present-day churches provide compelling testimony to this truth.

Strong, appropriate believers are promised a spirit of power and need to be supported to keep other believers wary and effective.[46]

Sabbath

Many of us have been taught that working or any other activity on Sunday interferes with setting aside that day to honor God and is against His moral code. These teachings have created significant guilt.

The mandatory Sabbath was discontinued when the Messiah made His first visit.[47]

Sensible living requires that we set aside a day of the week for worship and rest, but God doesn't require that we be legalistic about it.

Water Baptism

Baptism has been a source of church conflict for centuries and has caused the unfortunate dividing of many otherwise rational believers/seekers.

Some claim that baptism, by itself, guarantees life in Heaven. Some believe that once a person is baptized nothing, including continuous, willful, ungodly behavior, can change their heavenly destiny, that Heaven is guaranteed.

Others say that if the baptism method used is incorrect in their view (e.g. sprinkling versus immersion), the process is to no avail. Others claim that the age of the party being baptized is the critical factor and, especially, that one must be at least at the age of accountability for the process to be effective.

Some churches teach that if a person is not baptized their way, life in Heaven is not available, nor is leadership in their church. The result has been very damaging to God's programs. He surely mourns in Heaven as He sees these insignificant arguments harm His purposes.

God would have us be baptized as an acknowledgement of our commitment to and love for His ways.[48] It will bring us peace and joy if done in true faith. It is not a requirement. It is a gift of worship. It is a sacrament. It won't get us into nor keep us from Heaven.[48]

Works

Works is the concept that we can earn our way into Heaven by doing good things and/or by being good.[50]

The *only* opportunity for heavenly residence is through meeting the provisions of the atoning blood covenant fulfilled by the Messiah's perfect sacrifice.[51] We do this by acknowledging that we are sinners in need of that atonement and honestly repenting. We must believe in the Messiah and His redeeming work and commit ourselves to learning about Him and God's programs.

Many of us don't fully process this opportunity.[52] It doesn't make sense to us. We are used to an environment where we never receive something for nothing. Oh, some of us hear about God's program as youngsters, but by the time we have gone through the teen years, it's often forgotten unless we are really spiritually connected or lucky enough to have friends and family who can keep us on track.

More likely, the only method of going to Heaven, which most of us never really understood in our youth even if we heard about it, has been lost as we find ourselves in the pressure cooker of our peers and other life stresses. When we think about helping others under these circumstances, we are really responding to the pull of our consciences to do good. We substitute doing any kind of good for doing godly good as a kind of salve. Doing worldly good rather that godly good is fine, but it doesn't help us in our quest for a heavenly outcome for our afterlives, and in a hellish outcome, what's the difference how many good deeds we did while we were on earth?

Good deeds do count for something because at judgement time rewards are given for good deeds and punishment for bad deeds.[53] But we have to get to Heaven before rewards can be given and that cannot be done without first knowing and accepting the Messiah.

A measure of actually knowing Him is the good deeds we do once we accept Him because it's impossible, once we know Him, not to do good deeds.[54]

Notes, Chapter 4

1 Num. 11:1, NL
2 Eph. 4:26, NL
3 Num. 22–25, DK
4 Num. 22:19, DK; Num. 23:10, DK; Num. 23:28, Jude 11, DK
5 Rom. 1: 29–31, DK
6 2 Tim. 3:2–8, DK
7 Matt. 10:16, NL; Matt. 7:20, NL
8 Matt. 7:21–23, NL
9 John 3:3, DK
10 Job 5:17, NL; Prov. 3:11, NL; Heb. 12:5–9, NL; 1 Pet. 5:8, NL
11 Deut. 32:21, NL; Rom. 10:19–20, NL
12 Dake Bible, OT page 237, col. 3 & 4 "Backsliding"
13 2 Cor. 5:17–8, NL
14 1 Cor. 11:23–6, NL
15 Lev. 17:11, NL; Heb. 9:22, 10:4, NL
16 Lev. 1:4, NL
17 Isa. 52:135, 53:4–5, NL; Lev. 1:4, NL
18 Heb. 9:26, DK
19 Dan. 9:27, NL
20 Dake Bible, OT pages 632–3, col. 1 "The Spirit World et. al."
21 Dake Bible, OT page 632, col. 2 note 3; OT page 633, col. 1 notes 3–4, 6; Mark 5:9, DK; Matt. 26:53, DK
22 Matt. 9:33–4, 10:1–8, 12:24–8, 25:41, DK
23 Prov. 21:5, NL; 2 Pet. 1:10, NL
24 Prov. 10:22, DK
25 Jer. 17:10, DK; 2 Cor. 9:6, DK
26 Smith, Marsha A. Ellis (Editor). *Holman Book of Charts.* (1984) pages 58–9
27 Rom. 1:21–32, DK; 2 Tim 3:2–9, DK
28 1 Sam. 16:14–23, DK; Jon. 12:6, DK; Num. 22–24, DK; Acts 5:1–11, DK
29 Rom. 7:15–25, DK
30 Rom. 3:23, DK
31 Acts 10:34, DK
32 1Cor. 10:13, DK
33 Isa. 48:16, DK; Dake Bible, NT page 280, col. 1 "The Trinity"
34 2 Cor. 1:21–22, 5:5, DK
35 Dake Bible, OT page 634, col. 3 notes 1–6
36 Deut. 30:19, DK; Dake Bible, NT page 264, bottom, "Free Moral Agency"

37 Rom. 2:12–15 NL; Dake
Bible, NT page 236, col.1
"Conscience"
38 Matt. 13: 18–23, NL
39 Luke 12:29, DK
40 Matt. 15:8–9, DK
41 Dake Bible, OT page 784,
"Election"
42 Rom. 2:12, DK
43 Dake Bible, NT page 284,
col. 3 note 21
44 Dake Bible, OT page 784,
"Election"
45 Eph. 6:10–18, NL
46 Eph. 6:10, DK
47 Dake Bible, OT page 119,
col. 3 "Sabbath"
48 Matt. 3:6, DK
49 Jon. 7:38, DK
50 Eph. 2:8–10, DK
51 Lev. 17:11, DK; Titus 3:5–7,
DK
52 Matt. 7:14, DK
53 1 Cor. 3:12–15, DK
54 James 2:17, NL

Abbreviations

DK   Dake Bible, Dake Publishing, Lawrenceville, GA
NL   New Living Study Bible, Tyndale House Publishers,
     Wheaton, IL
NT   New Testament
OT   Old Testament

Chapter 5

Lifestyles of Success

A s I HAVE MATURED in spiritual matters, I have found
many very helpful guidelines in God's Book that have
made my life much more palatable. I offer a concise version of these principals to you. I hope they will contribute to your
decision-making and well-being. They are obviously covered in
greater detail in the Bible.

Lending and Borrowing

God has no problem with lending and borrowing by contract
and he has no problem with responsible, collateralized debt.
These are classic tools of commerce in both business and personal life. Both parties are expected to be contractually protected
and benefited. If owed money is not paid, the lender is presumed
to have structured the contract so that he will come out whole,
and the borrower will suffer because of his inability to perform.
We are to always pay our debts in full in a timely way, or work
out an alternative with the lender.[1]

If believers undertake a bad deal, God expects us to see the
contract through.[2] He does permit honest renegotiation.

God does have problems with immoderate leverage, or overreaching safe and practical limits. Those limits depend on the
makeup of the individual, his family, and the conventions of the
business. God is not against making money or against comfortable living. He is against transactions that provide problematic

stress or distract the parties from spending balanced time with Him and others.

He does discourage co-signing, preferring that money be given away in expectation of responsible repayment.[3] If never repaid, the lender can presumably go on with life satisfactorily. That way, Satan has a smaller foothold if repayment is never received.

Communication

God intensely desires to communicate with us but He uses different methods than we do with each other. He doesn't talk with us audibly. We cannot look into His eyes or see His expression. We can't hear the tone of His voice.

Today, God and his messengers primarily communicate through

- thought impressions, visions, and dreams, especially during sleep, prayer, or study of His Bible,
- the still-small (i.e. inner) voice,
- thoughts triggered while in conversation with someone else, possibly on an altogether different subject,
- inputs from others whom we trust and who also know Him.[4]

He often authenticates His conversations by giving us confirmation from another of the above sources.

We need to train ourselves to be alert for these messages. We must develop a confidence about receiving them. Most importantly, we need to discern between messages from God and messages from Satan.[5]

God expects to hear from us via prayer and meditation on His word. It is through prayer and thinking about Him that we can place our needs, wants, and gratitude before Him.[6] This should be done personally, not through an intermediary. Sometimes we are hurting so much that we don't know how to pray for ourselves or our situations. Prayer support from others can be helpful, but it is not a substitute. Outside help should not be our primary method of communication. This is something we need to learn to do directly, and He is a gracious teacher.

Counsel

God advises us to get many counselors prior to making significant decisions.[7] Unfortunately, many of us fail to heed this advice, lack discernment in finding godly counselors, and fail to listen to the timely advice of God when the advice of counsel does not agree with what we feel inside after considerable prayer and pondering.

Getting sufficient and appropriate counsel takes a lot of time and slows down the decision-making process. This is often not popular or good for one's self-esteem. The flip side of this is being unable to act on wise and clear counsel once given; Satan loves to keep us in bondage.

A huge amount of counsel is available in our time, both for fee and for free. The idea that you get what you pay for is not always true when it comes to counsel. Discerning wise counsel is an art. It requires perception and engagement, purposeful thinking, prayer, and sometimes, just plain luck. We can be easily misled by the wicked, the ungodly, and occult spirits. The best advice is to be careful and patient, learning to listen to and trust our inner voices, and to look for collaborating coincidences.[8] We need to be watchful – not all inner voices come from godly sources.[9]

God will sometimes want us to act counter to even the finest and best-intentioned counsel. It takes a lot of experience, self-confidence, and courage to follow this lead.

Discernment

Discernment is perhaps one of the most necessary and valuable tools for success in life. To have it in full requires vast maturity in the soul and the spirit, the two everlasting components of a person.

The emotional, intellectual, and spiritual must be properly in balance for discernment to be strong. Weakness in any one of these three, especially the first and the last, will handicap a person so that serious decision errors will be made. Wholeness is rare. It is incumbent upon each person to get these three in balance, or to identify weak areas and rely on trustworthy counsel for assistance where weak. A commitment must then be made to include the recommendations of the counselor(s) in all serious matters. Few of us are fortunate enough to achieve quality levels of discernment in the majority of life's challenging areas.

Discernment applies to many areas of life including friendships, marriage, vocations, avocations, daily behavior choices, spirituality, and balance.

The simple fact that most of us do not discern the importance of the final choice we are making regarding our spiritual destiny is indicative of our profound weakness in discernment.

We must recognize that this is an area of life where Satan is very active in all of us.

Discipline and Moderation

One of the most difficult things for us to do, especially in our culture of plenty, is to withhold ourselves from things that are appealing. Social pressure often leads us into wrong behaviors or excesses and it keeps us away from things that are not socially popular.

God advises us to be moderate in all things.[10] This requires that the unnatural action of withholding be applied in most areas of life.

God also advises us to not offend others by our choices. That does not, however, mean that we should do wrong things just to please the crowd, just that we are not to do things that make others uncomfortable.[11]

For example, God has not prohibited us from drinking wine. He does prohibit us from drunkenness and advises against strong drink.[12] If we cannot control overconsumption, we may need to not drink alcohol at all. This can be extended to getting out of control in other types of substance abuse such as food, drugs, and sex.[13]

Also to be considered here is the misuse of our tongues. The Bible speaks of the tongue as being like the small rudder that steers the large ship. We must be vigilant against letting it lead us to evil things. The righteous understand how to properly use the tongue.[14]

The byword is to be moderate in all that we do, otherwise we may be in sin. Spiritual development requires the discipline of withholding.

Dispute Resolution

The biblical process for the resolution of conflicts and disputes is outlined in Matthew 18. It involves the use of spiritually likeminded independent arbitrators. This process is also being heavily utilized today in secular dispute resolution due to the high costs and poor results of litigation. Most successful businesses utilize a formal dispute resolution policy embracing arbitration as a required process for most matters. Of course, in secular situations the requirement for spiritual like-mindedness is omitted.

Likewise, in personal relationship issues, this process is being used more and more. Unfortunately, the believer community does not use it as effectively as it should.

Sometimes we also see believers who attempt to hide behind Matthew 18 to avoid necessary conflict.

Fear

Fear is widely discussed in the Bible. Two primary kinds of fear are especially important to understand.

The first is the admonition to fear the Lord. When the Bible says to fear the Lord, it really means to hold Him in profound reverential trust and awe.[15] It's important to realize that God is not someone to fear, but should be viewed as our kindly Father, because that is who He is. To be fearful of Him just supplies support to Satan's programs. We must be aware, but not fearful of, Satan in every activity of our lives.

I suggest that when reading the Bible in the future, you simply substitute the phrase "profound reverential trust and awe" when seeing the word fear in reference to God, and the true meaning of the passage will become clear.

We do want to focus on the second kind of fear: the emotion of irrationally feeling extreme danger. Basically, God tells the believer not to feel fear, that God is in control and watching over the moderately behaving believer and that He cares about every part of us and every situation we encounter to the extent of numbering the hairs on our heads.[16]

Going through life feeling fearful about things boils down to either faithlessness in God or an absence of knowledge.[17] If one lives life in fear, more biblical study will be helpful. When we know God, nothing in this life will frighten us for long.

We can tell when we have fear under control because our spirits are full of boldness, power, love, understanding, logical thinking, and moderation.[18] If we are living in fear, the other side has the control and we witness the opposite of the above.

Forgiveness

Giving forgiveness to others is a requirement for receiving forgiveness from God.[19] It is also necessary for our own mental and emotional health.

Acknowledgement of wrongdoing by the wrongdoer is unnecessary for the act to benefit the forgiver. Forgiveness can be offered without that acknowledgement, to the benefit of the forgiver.

However, relationship health is unlikely to improve unless the offender works toward ownership and positive change. Sometimes, the offended must show patience, even for years.

Unfortunately, we cling to our hurts. We also tend to cling to our own dysfunctional behaviors, behaviors that have previously led us into trouble. The Bible calls these behaviors "broken cisterns," a metaphor for mankind's substituting its own devices for God's programs for problem resolution and His grace.[20] This leads to emotional and spiritual impairment. Ultimately, it empowers the ineffective programs of the dark side.

Most of us forgive so infrequently and/or so ineffectively that we never experience the joy that comes from truly leaving something hurtful by the wayside. Rather, we want to reverse the Golden Rule, to do evil for evil, which God says is wrong. The practice of an eye for an eye and a tooth for a tooth didn't carry into our covenant period. God provides ultimate vengeance.[21]

For His part, God tells us He will blot out our sins from his mind and record book when we get right with Him.[22] We need to learn to do the same thing in our interpersonal relations that He does for us. This is easy to say, but difficult to do.

Forgetting

Forgetting is another matter. We are not commanded to forget the wrongdoing of others unless they have truly repented and made permanent changes in their lives. To forget without these changes being confirmed will often unwisely open a healthy person to further harm from an insincere or unwilling malefactor.

Evidence of true repentance or change on the part of a malefactor is often sporadic and inconclusive. One of the major trials of life is to work these situations out.

We are admonished to "forget those things which are behind." This becomes even more effective when we recognize that this advice applies to forgetting both our own past mistakes and the mistakes of others so that we can move forward in self-improvement. In a word, it means to not let Satan keep us so wounded about the mistakes of our past that we cannot grow in God.

Giving

God requires our acknowledgement of Him in one of the most personal and difficult of all areas, finances. However, many of us are sick and tired of dealing with spiritual leaders who sometimes seem more interested in our pocketbooks than our souls. Where is the balance? What is our financial calling and why?

The Bible says that ultimately, everything is God's. We merely get to use His things for awhile. If we want to be in line with His principles, He expects us to give a minimum of 10 percent of our new income to His earthly representatives to be used for His purposes.[23] Gifts, called offerings, are also welcome on top of that if we wish. We can give more than 10 percent if we feel called to. Above all else, He doesn't want us to give anything unless we are cheerful about it.[24]

If we honor this guideline, He promises to give us overflowing blessings.[25] Not always immediately, as we are so used to having things in our instant-gratification world, but timed as He knows is best for the development of spirituality in ourselves and those around us.

Why wouldn't everyone take this deal if they believe in God and are serious about Him?

The problem is that most of us are so protective of our finances that money becomes our god. For example, the rich young ruler spoken of in Matthew 19 represents a condition common to every generation. The Scripture does not tell us that the young ruler was to sell and give all of his possessions away, rather to sell them and give (but not necessarily give all) to the poor. Giving all would only be necessary if retaining some of his possessions made it impossible for him to tune in to God.

The only conditions that harmonize with the rest of Scripture are for him to sell that which would be necessary to meet the tithing portion of the covenant or to simply get the possessions in some form that would not obstruct his progress with God.

But that amount of money or that change was too much for this young man. Like many, he loved the practice of religion, but deep down where it really counts, he was unwilling to fulfill the minimal financial requirements. Money was his god. We don't know for certain what happened with him, except that he rejected the instruction to sever himself from his idol (his money). By doing so, unless he repented later, he also severed himself from a heavenly future at the same time.

Likewise, some like to give to "worthy" causes not involving God and count that giving toward the 10 percent. Unless these causes are for God's programs, they don't apply to the 10-percent covenant.

Some teach that the tithe is not a requirement during our covenant. Certainly they agree that something must be given. Why quibble or search for ways to reduce the amount? It's small enough anyway. Why run the risk of shortchanging God?

Since we either spend or save everything we get, our giving should usually be made at the time of income receipt, just like any other bill, so that we are not tempted to later withhold our payment to God.

If we cannot find immediate recipients that we deem worthy of our entire tithes, there are methods of "parking" a portion of

God's money legally while removing it from our access until a deserving purpose can be found. When using this method, we must make sure that we are not tempted into later using His money for some inappropriate purpose.

Marriage and Sex

For most of us, the single most tricky and important decision in life is mate selection. Yet many of us, including me, have failed miserably at this. Divorce rates are above 50 percent, even among believers, and they get higher yet with each successive remarriage. Why is mate selection so difficult? Where is God in this?

The problems originate with premarital behavior. Satan has been able to focus our culture on sexuality and lust to the extent that the exposure is so intense that it has destroyed our morality. All we need to do is watch television to see that this focus starts with our children at grade-school age. By the time they are in their teens, they are far down the slippery slope and there is little hope for reversing this problem for the balance of their lives.

The problem is that, once into this lifestyle, it's nearly impossible to stop. It is as consuming as the worst of addictions. For some it is possible to recognize the sin, atone for it, and make every effort not to sin again – God does willingly forgive. But that path is logically much, much more difficult than to avoid the behavior in the first place. The problem is that, except for the very disciplined, avoiding these situations is pretty much just wishful thinking in our culture of today.

So what can we do? Only our true best as we come into an understanding of knowledge and believe in God's promise that he will not allow us to be placed in temptation beyond our means to escape. Then, repent, learn, avoid those situations in the future, forgive ourselves after asking God's forgiveness, and go on.

The female seeks a secure, honest, open relationship with an affectionate, conversational male with whom to jointly build a family. The male desires a partner who is pleased to be in sexual fulfillment with him, takes care of her appearance, enjoys joining him in recreational activities, willingly takes care of the home, and sincerely admires him. But these aspirations are hard to achieve.

In our society, where we have so much sexuality constantly poured over us by the media, we start out life with liabilities that don't disappear later. This propagates all sorts of problems. One of them is divorce. Divorce is a moral problem that is a heavy contributor to the failing of our society.

A literal and conservative interpretation of the Bible provides only two acceptable reasons for the option of divorce. The first is continual, unrepentant immorality on the part of one of the partners.[26] Here we are talking about sustained sexual misconduct, not a quick one-night or one-weekend mistake, unless that behavior repeats itself regularly with different partners. Believers need to forgive their partners' mistakes, unless they are repetitive.

The second acceptable reason for divorce is when a believer is married to an unbeliever and the unbeliever chooses to voluntarily and permanently leave the believer without any pressure from the believer.[27] God provides for no other crystal clear grounds for initiating divorce, although divorces occurring prior to becoming born again are forgiven under the "new person" provision.

Likewise, God treats homosexuality as a (forgivable) sin.[28]

We can overcome our sexual sin, but it takes initiative and hard work. Many times we are simply unwilling to exercise our free will in favor of God's teaching in these matters. Balaam's trick of seducing the unaware into sexual sin in order for them to receive God's disfavor is very much in play today.

Never Early, Never Late

One of the more frustrating things we need to get used to when dealing with God is that He never operates on our time schedule. We are used to instant gratification. He is used to moving after testing faith or as it will impact other situations that we may be unaware of.

If one wants to avoid discouragement with God, it is mandatory to acknowledge that, according to His schedule, He is always on time. Because it amounts to giving up a certain amount of control, this can be highly frustrating until we get used to it. Then it can bring peace.

Overcoming

A fundamental challenge of our lives is to overcome the pressures of this world and the influence of the spiritual powers of darkness in order to achieve Heaven rather than Hell. Overcoming is a choice, our individual choice. God can't do it for us, and neither can anyone else. We all have the ability to overcome, but it takes intention, commitment, and sustained effort. It is only by recognizing the severity of the challenge, enlisting God's help, and putting into our life walk the tools necessary for success that it is possible to make it. It will not just happen. Revelation 2, 3, and 21 illustrate this point clearly.

Repentance

Since we are simply unable to stop sinning, we must be continuously repenting.[29] The practice of regular repentance serves as a reminder of our true natures. It establishes a healthy perspective on how we must relate to God so that in good times we don't let our human righteousness cause us to forget our abject powerlessness to stop behaving in violation of God's will.

Reaching the Spiritually Lost

The spiritually lost fall into several major groups. The following categories are of interest to us here:

- individuals previously hurt by Christians who are now turned off
- individuals raised in a family environment where some form of spirituality other than the uncompromised Bible was taught
- the spiritually misdirected
- those who have never heard the truth of the biblical message

Many in these groups have an interest in understanding the truth. When believers meet someone who states that they are not interested in more knowledge regarding biblical conclusions, it is wise to discover why. Unfortunately, many who believe get critical and judgmental with such people instead. They rave about their spiritual beliefs, rather than attempting to get the seeker to open up regarding the source of their hurts or the cultural experience that keeps them closed. This approach of the believing community, and the hypocrisy the outsiders see, simply confirms the correctness of their conclusions regarding believer hypocrisy. This is sad and unfortunate.

Study

It's important to study the Bible on our own. It works best when we do this for at least ten minutes daily, or as often as possible, and early in the day. Within thirty days, most people conclude that studying the Bible is an overall time-saver.

No one else can do this for us. Group work is good, but the best progress can be made one-on-one with Him. It's best to study a present-day language version of the Bible, not King James.

For females, the gospel of John is usually a great place to start because it is very diverse. For males, Romans is usually better as it is more compartmentalized. To study, of course, implies a depth of effort beyond normal quick reading. Try it! Peace and understanding will gradually be achieved.

Also, learn to pray. Larry Lea's book *Could You Not Tarry One Hour* is helpful. It is available on tape, too.

Summary

What are we to accomplish during our lives? Most of us have little, if any, awareness of the individuals of two generations past in our own families. Almost no evidence of our lives will exist on the face of the earth a century after we are gone. How can that be? All of the emotions, efforts, and accomplishments of a lifetime are almost totally forgotten, just like that. How tragic!

Intuitively, we know that there must be more to life. The laborious results of a life well lived can count for something lasting. The pain that we endure, physical, emotional, and mental, should have some permanent and worthwhile value.

But many of us get duped out of that value. How? By not acknowledging God's interest in us as our *personal* Father, a Father who cares so much for our eternal destiny that He may let us endure pain and suffering authored by Satan if it will help us or someone else come to Him.[30] These events often cause us to become seekers, which will result in heavenly rewards, rather than perpetual and eternal pain.[31]

Notes, Chapter 5

1   2 Kings 4:7, NL; Rom. 13:8, NL
2   Pss. 15:4, DK
3   Prov. 17:18, NL
4   Dake Bible, NT page 157, col. 2 "8 Ways God Speaks"; 1 John 4:1, DK
5   1 John 4:1, NL
6   1 Sam. 1:27, DK; Dake Bible, OT page 633, col. 2–3 "The Providence of God"
7   Prov. 15:22, 24:6, NL
8   Dake Bible, NT page 157, col. 2–3 "8 Ways God Speaks"
9   Luke 12:29, DK
10   Phil. 4:5, DK
11   Rom. 14:21, DK; Hag. 2:13, Amplified Bible
12   Dake Bible, NT page 222, col. 4 "Christian Law on Drinks"; Rom. 13:13, DK; Gal. 5:19–21, DK; Isa. 5:11, DK
13   Prov. 23:21, DK; 1 Tim. 2:9, DK
14   Prov. 10:32, DK
15   Prov. 1:7, DK
16   Pss. 112:7, DK; 2 Tim. 1:7, DK; Luke 12:7, DK
17   Mark 4:40, DK
18   2 Tim. 1:7, DK
19   Mark 11:25, DK
20   Jer. 2:13, DK
21   Deut. 32:35, DK; Heb. 10:30,1, DK
22   Acts 3:19, DK
23   Mal.3:8, DK; 2 Cor. 8:12, 9:6–8, DK
24   2 Cor. 9:7, DK
25   Luke 6:38, DK
26   Matt. 5:32, DK
27   1 Cor. 7:15, DK
28   Rom. 1:26–28, DK
29   Rom. 7:15–25, NL; Mark 1:5, DK
30   Jon. 9: 1–3, NL
31   1 Cor. 3:13–15, DK

Abbreviations

DK   Dake Bible, Dake Publishing, Lawrenceville, GA
NL   New Living Study Bible, Tyndale House Publishers, Wheaton, IL
NT   New Testament
OT   Old Testament

God's Plan for the Ages

Introduction to Part Two

MOST OF US DESIRE more peace, happiness, security and beauty in our lives. These things come out of knowing who we are inside, which brings contentment and surety about things. At the end of the day, this always comes down to spirituality. Not religion, but spirituality.

God is certainly aware that one of the most significant obstacles to knowing Him is understanding his programs in conjunction with a perspective of time. God, like all parents, is familiar with the frustration for both parent and child when the latter do not have the experience, prudence, and understanding about the future that healthy parents have developed in their lives.

So it is with all of us in getting to a point of comprehending spiritual matters, in particular the future. Sure, there is a lot of information available on the topic, but most of it is meaningless to us due to the impossibility of sifting something useful out of the mass of information, the difficulty of expressing high spiritual concepts in everyday language, and the blockages caused by bad previous experiences. I, like most businessmen, like to really understand my environment. I have found that with study the environment of this life can become comprehensible, and laying things out on a timeline really helped me put it all together in my mind.

In the following chapters, I will attempt to straightforwardly present the history, programs, future, and timing of God as I have come to understand them in an unbiased and unstrained way in conjunction with other world events so that readers can easily understand and assess these matters for themselves. Certainly my particular interest in the future is common to my business nature. Understanding the past always sheds light on future events. Businessmen routinely have the time clock of future events clicking in the back of their heads. Business, that most interesting and complex of all games, is a game of survival with infinite variations. It is only by projecting the future and continuously revising plans that a business can survive.

Some of this content will be presented by inference from incomplete evidence or evidence about which there is some conjecture. My intent is to present material fairly so that a logical conclusion can be determined by each reader.

This is not intended to be an academic presentation. It is hoped that the reader will consider it a well-researched summarization of the facts we have available in early 2000.

Chapter 6

Our God of Covenants

A s I BEGAN MY JOURNEY toward understanding God, I found that He operates under covenants, or "deals." These covenants have a duration, one flowing into another. One of the early deals He made was to utilize angels to govern His creation. Satan got the earth, which he was to rule on behalf of God.[1] Satan and the other ruling angels were given the same gift of free will that we are.[2] Satan rebelled against God in an attempt to become supreme over God, taking one-third of the angels with him.[3]

Even though Satan broke the covenant, God did not suspend His covenant. Why? Perhaps because God wants to fulfill His entire plan, which includes human resurrection. This covenant permits Satan to maintain certain limited and temporary rulership rights over the earth. This covenant has not expired yet, but will, and probably soon. We know the conditions necessary and they appear near. We just do not know the specific timing.

God has many purposes in permitting Satan to exist, including:

- to afflict people to bring us to repentance
- so that believers can be rewarded later by overcoming conflict while here
- so that believers can develop strength, character, and faith
- so that God's power over Satan can be demonstrated[4]

To understand the topic of covenants it should be remembered that all of God's promises have two major caveats. The first is contractual adherence – God never violates any conditions of his agreements.

The second is that God's promises always carry with them conditions. He will do such and such *if* we do such and such. Most of the confusion and disappointment mankind, and especially the Hebrews, have had with God centers around the unwillingness to follow through on our responsibilities in order to enjoy God's promises.[5]

God has many covenant periods in his overall plan for the world.[6] In each covenant period, God offers an agreement between Himself and mankind that has its own unique elements. We will cover seven covenants starting with Adam and ending with the millennium, which follows that great battle known as Armageddon.

The Covenant of Innocence

The first covenant period of this era immediately followed Satan's flood. (See pages 32–33, 89.) It commenced with the time of Adam and Eve's existence in the Garden of Eden prior to their disobedience. This may be called the Covenant of Innocence. During this time God provided for all of their needs and they were unaware of good and evil. When they fell into sin, this covenant ended.[7]

The Covenant of Conscience

The next period ran for about 1650 years through the end of the flood of Noah. It could be called the Covenant of Conscience. Mankind was on their own to listen solely to their consciences regarding behavior. Unfortunately, humans did poorly without stronger direction from God, and civilization (except plant and animal life and eight humans) had to be destroyed during the flood of Noah.[8]

Human Government

Following that period came 427 years during which human government prevailed. Nimrod was the world ruler during this period, which ended with another rebellion against God and the destruction of the tower of Babel (in present-day Iraq).[9] As punishment, God introduced different languages. This model was also a failure due to the evil behavior of the human leadership.

The Covenant of Faith

Next God patiently offered a new deal that we could call the Covenant of Faith or Promise. This period was characterized by the life and works of Abraham, his successors, and followers.[10] They came to God by faith, or by believing in Him even though they could not actually see Him. This period lasted 430 years until the time of the Exodus from Egypt. It came to an end when God observed that faith without a few simple written rules was not enough to keep people in line with His program. It is important to recognize that this original program of faith, to be repeated later as a significant component of our present covenant, came before the time of the Law.

The Law

The next period, covering over seventeen hundred years, was the period of the Law (of Moses) which lasted until the time of Christ. During this period, a formula of laws was given, which was designed to help people behave at a level matching God's standards.[11] The Law failed also. Today, many Hebrews cling to components of that covenant period.

The Covenant of Grace

We now live in the Covenant period of Grace, a time when we have been given a reminder of the written and only certain method by which we can get to Heaven even though we sin frequently.[12] As in all of the previous covenants, this deal has its own unique components put in place by God. Some of the conditions of the previous covenants, as usual, carry over. But not all. We have our free will intact so that we can choose, as before. We don't know exactly how long this covenant period will last, but it has already lasted longer than any previous covenant period.[13]

Divine Government

What follows this period is a covenant that might be called Divine Government, also called the millennium. This period will last one thousand years. It is a period during which the Messiah will live and reign on earth.[14] During this time preparations are made for the later coming of God to reside on earth. Eternity follows this period.

Notes, Chapter 6

1 Dake Bible, OT page 634, col. 1 "Satan First Ruler of Earth"; Ezek. 28:11–19, DK
2 Dake Bible, OT page 633, col. 4 "What He Is"
3 Isa. 14:12–15, NL
4 Dake Bible, OT page 634, col. 4 "God's Purpose in Allowing"
5 Dake Bible, NT page 284, col. 3 note 21
6 Dake Bible, OT page 53, col. 3 "30-fold Dispensational Plan"
7 Gen. 3:24, DK
8 Gen. 6:5, NL; Gen. 7: 10–24, NL
9 Gen. 10:9, NL; Gen. 11:4–5, DK
10 Gen. 12:1–Exod. 12:36, DK
11 Exod. 12:38, DK; Matt. 3:1, DK
12 Matt. 3–Rev. 19, DK
13 Dake Bible, OT page 61, col. 2 "Dispensation of Grace"
14 Dake Bible, OT page 61, col. 4 "Divine Government"

Abbreviations

DK Dake Bible, Dake Publishing, Lawrenceville, GA
NL New Living Study Bible, Tyndale House Publishers, Wheaton, IL
NT New Testament
OT Old Testament

Chapter 7

The Eternal Past

G OD STARTS GIVING US something concrete to work with about 4200 B.C. with the commencement of the record of the Bible.[1] Prior to that we can speculate about history, lifestyles, and spirituality with some level of success, but written facts are sketchy. Perhaps one of the most interesting books available for the layman on prebiblical conditions is James Michener's *The Source*. He provides what seems to be a plausible scenario for lifestyles and possible events of that earlier time.

But in order for us to proceed on our quest to understand spirituality and thereby bring peace into our lives, we don't need perfect historical detail. Fossil history makes it clear that a civilization of some sort involving animals, vegetation, and man-like creatures existed long before Genesis 1:3. The Bible can be understood to be in harmony with those findings. (See pages 32–33.)

It is during these long-ago years and with these long-ago human creatures, spoken of by Michener and discovered as fossils, that human spiritual life commenced when Satan became the angelic ruler of the earth. Desiring to be worshiped as God, Satan eventually rebelled against God as a result of his pride and took one-third of the other angels of Heaven with him. Satan's evil personality had been copied on earth. As the earth had become too evil and ungodly, God chose to destroy it with the flood of Satan recorded in Genesis 1:2.

Following the re-creation events of Genesis 1:3 and subsequent, Satan was able to retain certain rights on earth after the fall of Adam and Eve in the Garden of Eden. The covenant right to appear in the Court of Heaven to criticize and challenge the legitimacy of would-be followers of God was also maintained.[2] The period during which Satan has this privilege is now rapidly coming to a close, as we shall see.

Chart 1

4200 B.C.   **4000 B.C.**

EARLY AGES – ADAM AND EVE

Genesis 1:3 and subsequent recreation of the earth
Replenishment of the earth
Adam names the animals
    Eve created
    The fall of Adam and Eve
    Satan regains limited rights
      Abel – Cain
        Substitutionary blood atonement
        introduced
          Giants

Destruction – Satan's Flood

Gen 1:2

THE ETERNAL PAST

Genesis 1:1
Original creation of earth
Reign of Satan

    Early evil mankind
      Fossil history
        Satan's rebellion with
        one-third of the angels

COVENANT OF CONSCIENCE

COVENANT PERIOD: **PRE-ADAMITE COVENANT**

Notes, Chapter 7

1   Dake Bible, OT page 51, col.
    4 "15 Things the Bible
    Does Not Say"
2   Job 1 & 2, DK

Abbreviations

DK   Dake Bible, Dake Publishing, Lawrenceville, GA
NL   New Living Study Bible, Tyndale House Publishers,
     Wheaton, IL
NT   New Testament
OT   Old Testament

Chapter 8

The Early Ages

A BOUT 4200 B.C. the events of Genesis 1:3 and subsequent
began. Adam, Eve, and animal life were reestablished and
the replenishment of the earth was commenced. They
lived a nirvana-like life briefly, as they were in complete harmony
with and totally taken care of by God.

This period soon ended, however, when they chose to directly
disobey God by consuming the fruit of the tree of the knowledge
of good and evil.[1] It may seem overly strict to us that God would
punish them so tragically over what seems to be such a small
matter. What is the big deal about eating a particular fruit,
anyway? But God requires us to be sinless, which can only come
with obedience. This may make us chafe, but we didn't write the
rule book.

This was the first sin of our new creation and it resulted from
the weak wills of Adam and Eve. However, this was not the first
time God had experienced Satan-originated sin from mankind.
Satan's purpose in this new deception was to take over the minds
and hearts of mankind to serve his plan of eventually developing
enough resources to defeat God and take over His role of Supreme
Being.[2] Satan presently has certain limited rights over mankind
to challenge the spirituality of those seeking God while building
his own team of followers.[3] There will ultimately be, as we will
see later, a final conflict on earth that will permanently bring conclusion to this centuries-old conflict between God and Satan.

God's long-term purpose is to allow individuals who are truly
serious about a relationship with Him to choose everlasting life

with Him, which will eventually be in a form similar to the pre-fall times enjoyed by Adam and Eve.

Two of Adam and Eve's sons chose different vocations: Abel was a hunter, Cain a farmer.[4] God required gifts be given to Him as acknowledgement of his rulership. God determined that the blood sacrifice of a perfect animal was the sole means of atonement for sin.[5] God expected absolute obedience to this requirement. Since Cain was a farmer, he disliked the fact that God would not accept the products of his labor for the sacrifice and refused to give the prescribed blood – a second example of disobedience. Ultimately, in his jealousy and anger, he killed his brother, who was properly sacrificing. God permitted Abel's death as a lesson for mankind. Abel got something better in exchange for the brevity of his earthly life: eternal life in Heaven. Cain, unless he repented, obviously ended up in Hell.

This was also the time of giants. Giants were the result of sexual contact between fallen angels of Satan and human women.[6] God disapproved of this. These giants became a weapon of Satan.

Enoch was born in the 3600–3500 B.C. timeframe. Adam died in the 3300–3200 B.C. period. Shortly after Adam's death the earth saw the first known predeath rapture, or "snatching-up" to Heaven. Enoch was a man who "walked with God," or in other words, obeyed Him, while on earth.[7] He was translated alive to Heaven. This will become important later. Mankind is only appointed "once to die," and Enoch will probably be a member of a very important, small, and powerful group that will appear just before the close of this age.[8]

Noah was then born around 3150 B.C. and with this we have the conclusion of this millennium.[9]

Chart 2

4000 B.C.	3500 B.C.	3000 B.C.

EARLY AGES

ENOCH

NOAH

Enoch born

Methuselah born

Adam dies

Enoch raptured

Noah born

COVENANT PERIOD: **COVENANT OF CONSCIENCE** (cont.)

Notes, Chapter 8

1   Gen. 3, NL
2   Isa. 14: 13–14, DK
3   Job 1&2, DK
4   Gen. 4:1–17, DK
5   Gen. 4:4–5, DK
6   Dake Bible, OT page 62, col. 2 "Giants and Sons of God"
7   Gen. 5:24, DK
8   Heb. 9:27, NL
9   Gen. 5:29, NL

Abbreviations

DK   Dake Bible, Dake Publishing, Lawrenceville, GA
NL   New Living Study Bible, Tyndale House Publishers, Wheaton, IL
NT   New Testament
OT   Old Testament

Chapter 9

Noah

DURING THE NEXT MILLENNIUM, between 2600–2500 B.C., the development of papyrus for writing purposes occurred. Significantly, this technology would enable the permanent recording of God's programs for the first time, as opposed the storytelling method of transmission.

Of additional significance, it was the era of Noah. Noah was another godly man, but during his time there was another massive movement toward wide-spread evil. Eventually, things got so bad that God saw that the earth needed, once more, to be cleansed and restarted.[1] He accomplished that purpose by means of the flood of Noah about 2500 B.C. Only eight human souls were left worthy of saving, Noah, his wife, and their three sons and their wives.[2]

Satan's covenant continued after the flood just as before, but perhaps with some additional restrictions – we don't know for sure. God promised this would be the last judgement by flood and provided the rainbow as a sign of this promise.[3] The next judgement will be by fire, as predicted in Revelation.

Shem, one of Noah's sons, left the ark with his godly wife and began to populate northern Iraq, Iran, and Syria. Ham, another son, moved his family to southern Iraq, Israel, and northern Africa. Japeth and his wife populated Europe, Russia, Turkey, Greece, and northern Syria.[4] We are all progeny of these peoples.

During the 2200–2100 B.C. timeframe, pyramid construction started in Egypt. In Babylon, which is in present-day Iraq, Nimrod and his wife, Semiramis, came into power.[5] He was a successful hunter, warrior, and military leader under whose leadership false religion prospered. His tower of Babel was an earthly attempt to be "like God." This movement was led from the spiritual world by Satan.[6] The tower was a failure, and as a consequence of building it God confused the tongue of mankind by propagating the different languages that we suffer with today.

The Babylonian cult born by Nimrod and Semiramis included the worship of an incarnate Queen mother and her son. It is possible that future incarnate religions utilizing this model will link together just prior to the close of this age.

About this same time Abraham, father of Islam and the Judeo-Christian religions, began his migration to Israel at the command of God.[7] Abraham's great contribution was his belief in the unseen God. He had faith that God really existed. He was willing to trust his instincts about doing things God wanted him to do. Faith is the huge differential brought to mankind by Abraham. Faith is absolutely necessary for a relationship with God because He chooses to not make Himself visible at this time. Faith requires that we totally accept the validity of God's proposition, without many of our customary human devices for confirmation.[8]

Faith is not faith, but fact, if the proposition in question can be confirmed using all standard human faculties.

One way to support faith intellectually is the process we call reverse engineering. Reverse engineering was practiced recently in the Far East as a method for quickly copying and improving a product without the costly research and development required for altogether new products. It amounts to taking a finished product, breaking the product down into its smallest components, studying all aspects of the pieces, and by deduction building a substitute.

This same process can be applied in spiritual study. Faith does not need to be totally blind, it can be supported by rationale. All that is required is that we believe first, and then look backward to figure out how things got the way they did. The pieces will fall in place.

Faith is developed by hearing the word of God.[9] It has a component of expecting a rational, confirming, and complete outcome, and an element of confidence and certainty in the outcome. Faith replaces our worldly sight as we see things from a divine perspective.

Atonement and Substitution

Somewhat later, about 2050 B.C., God's earlier covenant providing for the temporary atonement for sins by the substitute sacrifice of a perfect animal was written down in Genesis 22 and Leviticus 17.

In the early days, before the Messiah, this was accomplished through the ritual of animal sacrifice as an interim measure pending the later arrival of the perfect substitute, the Messiah. Since the first coming of the Messiah, animal blood is no longer necessary because His perfect blood was given once and for all.[10] Today it is only necessary to appropriate that act of permanent atonement by individual assent (i.e. faith). It is only on the basis of claiming this provision that we can have a relationship with God both here on earth and then permanently in Heaven after the death of our bodies.[11] This causes all of our past, present, and future sin to be blotted out from our personal record books, making us acceptable to God as long as our successive sins are covered by repentance.[12]

Chart 3

3000 B.C.	2500 B.C.	2000 B.C.

EARLY BRONZE AGE

Mankind – evil once again

Early papyrus

Commitment of the rainbow
Shem – northern Iraq, Iran, Syria
Ham – Libya, northern Africa, Egypt, Ethiopia, Sudan, Israel
Japeth – Europe, Russia, Turkey, Greece, northern Syria

Pyramids
Babylon born – Nimrod

Tower of Babel cult
Abraham to Israel
Isaac
Substitutionary blood atonement recorded

Destruction – Noah's Flood

COVENANT PERIOD: **COVENANT OF CONSCIENCE** (cont.)   **COVENANT OF HUMAN GOVERNMENT**   **COVENANT OF FAITH**

Notes, Chapter 9

1   Gen. 6:11–13, NL
2   Gen. 7:7, NL
3   Gen. 9:13, NL
4   Dake Bible, OT page 40,
    col. 1–4 "Sons of Japeth,
    Shem & Ham"
5   Gen. 10:8, DK
6   Gen. 11:1–9, DK
7   Gen. 12:1–9, DK
8   Heb. 11:1–39, DK
9   Rom. 10:17, NL
10 Dake Bible, OT page 119,
    col. 1 "Atonement"; Job
    33:24, DK; Num. 17:11, DK;
    Heb. 9:22, DK
11 Exod. 29:10–14, DK; Lev.
    17:11, DK; Rom. 3:25, DK
12 Isa. 44:22, NL; Acts 3:19, NL

Abbreviations

DK   Dake Bible, Dake Publishing, Lawrenceville, GA
NL   New Living Study Bible, Tyndale House Publishers,
     Wheaton, IL
NT   New Testament
OT   Old Testament

Chapter 10

The Patriarchs

D URING THE EARLY PART of the next thousand years the first generation of God's chosen people, the Hebrews (the curators of His faith), began to propagate. Abraham was the patriarch. Simultaneously, the Arabic line, which would later produce Islam, emanated from the union between Abraham and Hagar, his wife's slave. Isaac and Jacob, Abraham's son and grandson through Sarah, fathered the line from which the Messiah was to come.[1]

Perhaps due to their early apostasy, or simply to enable the later fulfillment of God's programs, a famine befell the chosen people. To survive, Abraham's family had to migrate to Egypt, where they fell into slavery under the control of the Pharaoh for 430 years.[2] The bright side of this adversity was that the Hebrews developed into a huge nation while there.[3]

The Egyptian slavery situation is very important in terms of understanding God's predictions regarding the future for us. It commenced what is called the "Times of the Gentiles," a time when God, in order to chasten the Hebrews for choosing to disobey Him, caused the administration over the Hebrews to fall into the hands of gentiles.[4] We read extensively about this time in the early books of the Bible. We are still living in the Times of the Gentiles, but we are perhaps close to the climax of that era.

After developing from a small clan into a huge nation despite the extremely difficult circumstances of those 430 years, the Hebrews miraculously escaped Egypt under the leadership of Moses. Unfortunately, they had still not learned to follow God's ways, even after His extraordinary actions on their behalf. So He next gave them the written Law.[5] Unfortunately, this Law, which was designed to show the Hebrews the impossibility of behaving perfectly enough to be sinless and therefore eligible for eternal life, has become more of a culture than a religion that would help them adhere to His precepts. God desired to show them through the Law that only by means of His original program of faith in interim substitutionary blood atonement, followed by the (then future) coming of the Messiah, could they achieve Heaven. They did not, and have not, gotten it. Like Cain, they preferred their own program to God's.

Over the years, the Hebrews have added many interpretations to these basic laws, to the point where the whole thing is so convoluted that now even full-time scholars cannot comprehend it without disagreement. In fact, the world well knows the Hebrew affinity for argument. An old adage states, "Where there are two Hebrews, there will be at least three arguments."

Unfortunately, this has caused the average Hebrew of today to assign out the comprehension of God to "experts," or Rabbis. Without intending any dishonor to them, they are caught up for the most part in propagating only the first five books out of the sixty-six contained in the Bible, which has understandably led them to an incomplete understanding of the notions of the Book's Author. The result is that most present-day Hebrews don't even believe in an afterlife.

Job

Another important figure in this time was Job, who was, from an economic point of view, an early Bill Gates.[6] God provides the story of Job to teach us an understanding of God's purpose in allowing suffering in life and to be able to comprehend the present contractual relationship between God and Satan.[7] God gave mankind this information prior to giving the Hebrew "Law," perhaps in hope that the Law would not be necessary.

Why Suffering?

This was a topic of earthshaking interest to me because of our daughter's condition. I spent untold hours trying to figure out why we were in this situation. The following summarizes those findings.

We usually perceive God to be a benevolent supernatural spirit power. Why then do those who apparently provide allegiance to Him often suffer? Why do tiny, helpless children suffer? And, conversely, why do evil people often get away with things or avoid suffering? Does God cause these things? Or let them happen? Or isn't He involved? Is He too busy? Doesn't He care? And if so, why?

Many a believer or aspirant has asked these questions and many have become hurt or lost, unable to come up with satisfactory answers. Spiritual leaders from most denominations have offered their opinions, but most of us who have experienced substantial pain in our lives still don't have a peace in our spirits about their conclusions.

The answers are provided in God's Book. God may allow Satan to put us through suffering, trials, and chastening, if necessary to win us to His side or to put us in a situation where we consider Him.[8] The book of Job makes it clear that it is Satan, not God, who constantly accuses people of evil behavior and who works suffering and pain in their lives.[9]

Satan's Rights to Test

Satan has the right to challenge our spiritual destinies, even during our times.[10] We also read in Job 1 and 2 that Satan can negotiate for the right to destroy the property and harm the health of a good person. This can happen to a good person who has done nothing significantly wrong to deserve the test. (In Job's case the only infraction we know of is his operating in fear.[11]) We know that it is Satan, rather than God, who desires to do the harm to the individual because, as outlined elsewhere in the Bible, it is inconsistent with God's character to be the oppressor and Satan is identified as the oppressor in Job and other places.[12]

Suffering As an Example to Win Souls

Another reason God permits suffering is covered early in John 9. God relates to us by means of this story that the good can also suffer so that examples of godly behavior can be provided to those who don't know God.

Most of us can think of many present-era individuals who have suffered greatly but, as a result of that suffering, became great witnesses of courage and outreach for God. We may dislike this purpose, but it is not ours to choose. God's only goal is to win souls.

In both cases, God has reserved the right to limit the magnitude of Satan's tests.[13]

God's Purpose

God will permit suffering in His role of winning permanent life in Heaven for individuals. Recall that all of the apostles suffered. Jesus suffered. So why would we not suffer from time to time, as it helps God in soul-winning? This is, after all, a battle for the residency of our eternal spirits. This is the most serious event that will ever occur in the life of any individual, and there aren't any second chances.

When we become Heaven-focused, rather than earth-focused, we can begin to understand suffering. When we take on the perspective of a visitor to earth, with our permanent residence in Heaven, not here (what the Bible refers to as a sojourner), we can begin to achieve a correct outlook on this matter. This takes tremendous spiritual maturity. Until that status is achieved, we may not understand suffering.

Even if we can understand it, living it is entirely another matter. As I discovered with my daughter, it is only by the grace of God that certain things can be survived.

Many of us are somewhere along the path to righteous living. If we are not on the correct path, God may permit Satan's "sifting" to get us there.[14]

Other Events

Moses, a Hebrew child raised in the king of Egypt's home, was God's agent for changing the Israeli race. He led the Hebrews from captivity to freedom. He was the recipient of God's law. But because the Hebrew's faith in God was so weak, they were consigned to wander in the desert for forty years instead of moving immediately to their Promised Land. This was a great tragedy and a further illustration of their inability to just listen to and follow God's plan for them. Satan played a huge role in developing their fears and keeping the few who truly understood in check.

Finally, after the generation that lacked the faith to follow God's instruction to move into Israel had passed, God facilitated their entrance.[15] Moses' management team took over at his death, and God subsequently provided benevolent Judges for the rulership of Israel.

Control over them then passed from the Egyptians to the Syrians, who will most probably play a significant part in future events.

Toward the end of this millennium, the Hebrews complained incessantly about their leadership. They wanted Kings, rather than judges, just like the other nations. God told them (through their Prophets) that they would not like the results of that wish, but He honored their request nevertheless.[16] Saul became their first king.

Starting out as a godly man, Saul quickly fell into the backsliding behavior often common to leadership. As God predicted, he became a failure.[17] He was a tyrant, the people feared him, and they soon deduced that they simply had to live with it.

Chart 4

2000 B.C.	1500 B.C.	1000 B.C.
MIDDLE BRONZE AGE	**LATE BRONZE AGE**	**EARLY IRON AGE**

Jacob

Joseph

Job

Moses – The Law
Exodus
Torah (Pentateuch) and Job written

Saul

COVENANT PERIOD:
COVENANT OF FAITH (cont.)   **COVENANT OF LAW**

TIMES OF THE GENTILES:
EGYPT   **ASSYRIA**

ISRAELI RULE:
PATRIARCHS   **JUDGES**   **KINGS**

Notes, Chapter 10

[1]   Gen. 16:1–17:27, DK
[2]   Gen. 42:1–43:34, DK
[3]   Exod. 12:37, DK
[4]   Dake Bible OT page 873, col. 2 "Times of the Gentiles"; Luke 21:24, DK
[5]   Exod. 20–end, DK.
[6]   Gen. 46:13, DK
[7]   Job 1&2, DK
[8]   Dake Bible, NT page 259, col. 4 "Chastening"
[9]   Job 1:9–11, DK
[10] Luke 22:31, NL
[11] Job 3:25, NL
[12] Acts 10:38, DK
[13] Job 1:12, 2:6, DK
[14] Heb. 12:5–11, NL
[15] Josh. 1, NL
[16] 1 Sam. 8, DK
[17] Dake Bible, OT page 327, col. 4 "15 Steps in Saul's Downfall"

Abbreviations

DK   Dake Bible, Dake Publishing, Lawrenceville, GA
NL   New Living Study Bible, Tyndale House Publishers, Wheaton, IL
NT   New Testament
OT   Old Testament

Chapter 11

The Five-Empire Millennium

T HE NEXT MILLENNIUM commences during the continua-
tion of the Times of the Gentiles, with Assyria still on stage
as the world leader. David becomes king of Israel. In God's
eyes he is a good man because throughout his life he honors,
respects, and has faith in God. However, he is far from perfect.
He gets into sexual sin, he has times of weakness and fear, he is
nepotistic to a fault, and he loves to party.[1]

David wanted to build a swanky temple for God to replace
the portable tent temple built by Moses, perhaps in part because
he felt a little guilty about his own mansion. God told him that
he could not build the temple because of his violent background.
Nevertheless, God encouraged David to collect the materials for
the structure. It was later built by Solomon, David's son.[2]

A bit later, the prophet Elijah became only the second person
reported to be raptured to Heaven without dying.[3] He and Enoch
are the candidates most likely to be returned to earth to serve
God during the latter years of the Times of the Gentiles.[4] (See
page 150.)

To further set the context of this millennium, the *Iliad* and
the *Odyssey* appear at this time in Greek literature.

Soon the Babylonian empire unseated Assyria and, as part of
God's continued punishment for the Hebrews' disobedience,
became the third world empire to tread down the Hebrews.[5] God
permitted this because they still failed to honor Him and He was
tired of their dishonorable ways.

After destroying Jerusalem – and causing the first of two historically important dispersions of the Hebrews – the army of Babylonian king Nebuchadnezzar took a number of promising young Israelis to Babylon. Included was a Hebrew teenager named Daniel.[6] Daniel was to become one of the most important men of all time concerning the prophetic events that are soon to unfold in our future.

This was also the time of the prophet Isaiah, who provided us with the litmus test for false religions.

Validating Religions

Around 600 B.C., by means of inspiration from God, Isaiah recorded the only method provided by God to discern with certainty messages that are truly from Him, as opposed to falsehoods from those claiming to be God.

The litmus test is the accuracy of a prediction. Unless multiple future events can be perfectly foretold, the conclusion is that the predictions are not of God. And if not of God, they are from the other side. The predictions must occur perfectly, on target all of the time, not simply some of the time, and deal with complex, disassociated events over a period of time.[7]

The Bible presents over six thousand prophecies. Over half have already been perfectly fulfilled. The others are either presently underway or yet to come and are primarily associated with the "end-times," the millennium, and eternity.[8]

Since perfection has already been achieved every single time, fully as predicted, in more than half of the prophecies, there is little doubt that the remaining prophecies will be fulfilled perfectly, as well.

The writings of world religions not fully dependent on the Bible contain no such performance record. The test consists of the ability of the true religion to foretell the future perfectly. Only one religion in all the world can deliver on that challenge and that is the true religion of those who adhere to the Bible. Not the Hebrew religion, or denominational Christianity, or the Islam religion – just those who truly understand the straightforward teaching of the Bible absent all the doctrines of man inserted over the years.

The Eight Empires

Daniel, as mentioned earlier, was perhaps the most important prophet for our times. He is fascinating to me because he is so connected with future events. In him we discover a man gifted by God in the interpretation of dreams, both his own and others. One of the most important dreams processed by Daniel was the dream of King Nebuchadnezzar of Babylon, whom Daniel served. From that dream, Daniel understood the revelation of God regarding six world empires.[9] These six world empires were to follow the two Times of the Gentiles empires already past. These eight empires are to dominate Israel. The first two occurred prior to the time period covered by Nebuchadnezzer's first dream as interpreted by Daniel. The last two are yet to come.

- First Empire – Egyptian (at the time of Jacob, Joseph, and the Pharaoh)
- Second Empire – Assyrian
- Third Empire – Babylonian under Nebuchadnezzar's family (during Daniel's time)
- Fourth Empire – Medo-Persian
- Fifth Empire – Grecian (under Alexander the Great)
- Sixth Empire – Roman Empire (Effectively, the Roman Empire faded away over time and no other empire has since been established to rule over the old Roman/Grecian Empire territories, much less the entire world. We presently live during this time period, which is of indefinite length.)

- Seventh Empire – This will very likely be the European Economic Community (EEC) and a few Arabic nations. The future Antichrist will eventually become the ruler of this body of nations[10]
- Eighth Empire – This will be the final empire prior to the second coming of the Messiah. It will consist of the Seventh Empire and the balance of the countries that were a part of the Grecian Empire including at least parts of Afghanistan, Bangladesh, Burma, India, Iran, Nepal, Pakistan, Romania, Saudi Arabia, Syria, Turkey, Uzbekistan, Yemen, Yugoslavia, many other small counties, and perhaps even a small part of China[11]

Daniel's Dream

Daniel also interpreted an extremely important dream of his own regarding future events. In that dream, a period of seventy "heptads," or weeks of years, was revealed.[12] A week of years is seven years, so the vision covered 490 years (7 x 70). This vision was split into three primary periods.

Period One was seven heptads, or forty-nine years. This was the period from "the going forward of the commandment... to restore and to build Jerusalem." This commandment was given by King Artaxerxes of Persia to Nehemiah in 444 B.C.[13] Forty-nine years later, Jerusalem was restored and rebuilt under Nehemiah. This facilitated the first regathering of the Hebrews.[14]

Period Two was sixty-two heptads, or 434 years. It was to fall immediately after the first period. At the end of this period of 434 years "shall Messiah be cut off," or in other words, killed. Adjusting for the differences between the 360-day and the 364-day calendars, the exact date of the death of Yeshua (Jesus) results.

Period Three is one heptad, or seven years. It has come to be known as "Daniel's Seventieth Week."[15] It is one of the most important prophetic times given in the Bible. There is an indeterminate time between the death of Yeshua and the commencement of Daniel's Seventieth Week.[16] We are living in that indefinite time period right now.

Daniel's Seventieth Week is an end-times period, most likely coming soon, when the world as we know it will be drastically changed by events involving a powerful agent for evil known as the Antichrist and the events leading up to the battle of Armageddon.[17] This period is seven years in length and it immediately precedes the removal of Satan from the earth for one thousand years. The indefinite period of time between the death of the Messiah and Daniel's Seventieth Week is also known as the "church age."[18] This is a time God has provided for non-Hebrews in particular to come to an understanding of Him.[19] During this time, the Hebrews are to have a "veil" between them and God – not a wall, but a veil.[20] Once this period is over, the veil will disappear and God will once again embrace a close relationship with His chosen people, the Hebrews, and non-Hebrews will continue to have a normal status with Him.[21]

This seven-year period predicted by Daniel, sometimes called the tribulation period, is a time of particular difficulty on earth as millions are lost in battles, martyrdom, dramatic geophysical events, and cosmic struggles.[22] The final event of the battle of Armageddon in Israel will result in the defeat of the evil side when the Messiah makes his second complete return to earth.[23] (Prior to His final complete return for the battle He will make a partial return in the sky, known as the believer rapture, to meet those who claim His promises.[24])

Hebrews believe that this will be the first appearance of the Messiah, that He will come only once, and at that time, and as their King to defeat their oppressors once and for all. Christians believe that He was here as a servant once before and that He died in about A.D. 33. The Christian "believers" also agree that this (second) coming as King of the earth will occur. They only disagree with the Hebrews regarding whether this is His first or the second coming, and whether Yeshua was the Messiah or simply a prophet.

The book of Daniel is fundamental to understanding the world events soon upon us. We will refer to it repeatedly in chapter 14.

Simultaneous Secular World Events

In world history, by the mid-400s B.C. the Medo-Persian Empire took over from the Babylonian Empire. This was the time of Esther, who was the Hebrew Queen of Persia (Iran). Her role was significant in that she prevented the first attempted holocaust of the Hebrews by Satan's forces.[25] Satan's purpose was to cut off the line of the coming Messiah.

The first effective holocaust came during the time of Hitler, the second will come during the Seventieth Week predicted by Daniel.[26] It will also include a holocaust for gentile "believers."[27]

This was the time (469–399 B.C.) of Socrates, the Greek philosopher who was known for his opinions about moral and intellectual matters. Another Greek philosopher, Plato, was also on stage.

Alexander the Great of Greece took over as the fifth world emperor. His empire, like that of the Medes and Persians, was more easterly focused, going as far as parts of India and the southern countries of the former U.S.S.R. This was the "silent" period of the Bible, as we have little inspired writing available from 400 B.C. until the birth of Jesus.[28]

Alexander's empire was soon to fall to the Romans, whose focus was more northerly to Britain and westerly to Spain. Rome gave up territories east of Turkey, Iraq, and Syria. It is during this period that the now-famous community of Qumran was in full swing, Herod was king over Palestine, and Cleopatra was in Egypt.

Then, at the very end of this millennium, came the birth of Jesus.[29]

Chart 5

1000 B.C.	500 B.C.	0
MIDDLE IRON AGE	**LATE IRON AGE**	**GREEK PERIOD**

MIDDLE IRON AGE

David

Solomon – Temple

Elijah and his rapture
Jonah
Iliad and Odyssey

LATE IRON AGE

Alexander

Plato

Nebuchadnezzar
First dispersion
Daniel – 70 weeks
Isaiah – Ultimate test
Socrates
Esther
Nehemiah – Temple

GREEK PERIOD

Rome
Qumran
Herod
Cleopatra
Jesus
New Covenant
Julius Caesar

COVENANT PERIOD:
COVENANT OF GRACE

TIMES OF THE GENTILES:

ASSYRIA (cont.)	BABYLONIAN	MEDO-PERSIAN	GRECIAN	ROMAN

ISRAELI RULE:

KINGS	GENTILE

Notes, Chapter 11

1   2 Sam. 1–24, DK
2   1 Kings 1–11, DK
3   2 Kings 2:11, DK
4   Rev. 11:1–11, DK
5   2 Kings 24:1–25:30, DK
6   Dan. 1:6, DK
7   Isa. 41:23, NL; Isa. 42:9, NL
8   Walvoord, John. *Every Prophecy of the Bible.* (1999)
9   Dan. 2:1–49, DK
10   Dan. 7:23–24, DK; Dake Bible, chart 11
11   Dake Bible, OT page 877, col. 1 chart 10
12   Dan. 9:24–27, DK; Dake Bible, OT page 877, col. 3 "The 70 Weeks"
13   Dake Bible, OT page 878, col. 1 "The 70 Weeks, 6" (3)
14   Hos. 1:11, DK; Rev. 12:1, DK
15   Dake Bible, OT page 878, col. 1 note 11
16   Dake Bible, OT page 878, col. 1 note 7
17   Dan. 11:36–45, DK; Mic. 4:11, DK; Rev. 19:19, DK
18   Dake Bible, OT page 878, col. 1 note 10
19   Dake Bible, OT page 402, col. 4 note 37; Luke 2:32; Acts 26:15–18, DK; Rom. 3:29–30, NL
20   2 Cor. 3:14, DK; Rom. 11:25 DK
21   Zech. 12:10–13:9, DK
22   Deut. 31:29, DK; Dan. 11:40–12:1, DK; Matt. 24:21, DK; Rev. 7:14, DK
23   Rev. 19:11–21, DK
24   Matt. 24:30–31, DK
25   Esther 7–8, DK
26   Jer. 30:7, DK
27   Matt. 24:22, DK
28   Dake Bible, OT page 930, bottom, "Between the Testaments"
29   Matt. 1:1–25, DK; Luke, 2:1–35, DK

Abbreviations

DK   Dake Bible, Dake Publishing, Lawrenceville, GA
NL   New Living Study Bible, Tyndale House Publishers, Wheaton, IL
NT   New Testament
OT   Old Testament

Chapter 12

The Middle Ages

WITH JESUS came the New Covenant or, in our parlance, "better deal."[1] This better deal simply perfected the only path God has ever provided to mankind to spend eternity in Heaven, as opposed to the only other choice, Hell. God's arrangement for sin atonement, which is a requirement for a permanent relationship with Him in the form of eternal life, was articulated in writing during the time of Moses. This offer called for the periodic repentance of sin by the substitutionary sacrifice of a perfect and sinless animal interim to the coming of the Messiah.[2] The blood of the Messiah – when He came and if He could live and die flawlessly and not fall subject to Satan – would provide permanent and final atonement for all past, present, and future sin for all who would choose to acknowledge Him in their lives. Fortunately, He was able to accomplish His goal.[3] Now it is up to us individually.[4]

Jesus is considered by most Hebrews to be a prophet but not the Messiah, even in view of more than one hundred detailed and specific predictions from the Old Testament that could rationally apply only to Him.[5] Many Hebrews have grown to hate His name due in large part to the atrocities performed over the years by those who have supposedly followed His teachings.

At Jesus' death, He first went to a compartment in hell called Paradise and moved all inhabitants to Heaven.[6] These were the spirits of those whose bodies had already died but had trusted in God during their lives by showing faith prior to the actual coming of the Messiah. This compartment called Paradise now stands empty in Hell, as the spirits of those believers who have died since Jesus' death now go straight to Heaven.

Jesus returned to earth in visible spirit form on and off for about a month and a half after His bodily death.[7] His was the first permanent resurrection of any man.[8] After that month and a half, His presence on earth was replaced by the Holy Spirit.[9] The Spirit is still with us and will remain indefinitely to comfort and aid those seeking to understand God's truths.

Other Events

During His time on earth, Jesus trained disciples.[10] They continued His ministry after His death as itinerate ministers in many portions of the Roman Empire. John, one of His disciples, provides us much information in the book of Revelation about future events that is complementary to Daniel's work. Paul, a convert, does likewise in other books. Certain information comes from other old and new testament books as well.

In A.D. 70, thirty-seven years or so after Jesus' death, the Hebrew temple was again destroyed. This time it was accomplished by the Romans to punish the Hebrews for their rebellion against Rome.[11] For a second time the Hebrews were dispersed.

The final selections were made for the books of the New Testament during the third century A.D. Books that were candidates for inclusion but for various reasons didn't meet the test of divine inspiration or prophecy were excluded. Many of these books are now collected in the Apocrypha. The Apocrypha is also a good source of information about the Grecian Empire, which reigned during the Bible's "silent years" between 400 B.C. and the birth of Jesus.[12]

Next came the rapid growth of the Roman Catholic church, which separated the worship of God from the previous practice of worshipping the political head of the Roman Empire as being divine. This was soon followed in the seventh century A.D. by

Mohammed and the development of Islam. All four religions (Islam, Catholicism, Judaism, and Christianity) are biblically based.

By the time we come to the end of this millennium, papyrus has been replaced by paper and our world has substantially expanded beyond the environs of the near-Mediterranean countries. Rome ceased to be the world empire. Since then, no single government has been a world empire. But a new world empire will soon emerge, the definition of world in this case most likely being the same area meant by the term in the days of the Grecian and Roman Empires.[13]

Chart 6

0	A.D. 500	A.D. 1000

ROMAN PERIOD

MIDDLE AGES

Jesus died
Paradise and Jesus raptured
Holy Spirit
Disciples

Council of Nicaea/Carthage (NT fixed)

Roman Catholicism – Holy Roman Empire

Temple destroyed – Titus
Second dispersion
Paul
John – Revelation

Crusades

Mohammed – Islam

Paper replaces papyrus

Church Age Starts

WORLD

COVENANT PERIOD:
COVENANT OF GRACE (cont.)

TIMES OF THE GENTILES:
ROMAN

ISRAELI RULE:
GENTILE

Notes, Chapter 12

1 Heb. 8:1–13, DK; Rom. 3:21–4:17, DK
2 Lev. 17:11, DK
3 Rom. 1:16–17, NL
4 Deut. 30:19, DK; Dake Bible, NT page 264, bottom, "Free Moral Agent"
5 Smith, Marsha A. Ellis (Editor). *Holman Book of Biblical Charts.* (1984) page 58–9
6 Luke 16:22, DK
7 Acts 1:3, 1:9, DK
8 1 Cor. 15:20–23, DK; Matt. 9:25, DK
9 Acts 2:1–21, NL
10 Matt. 5:1–28:20, NL; Mark, 1:1–15:18, NL; Luke 5:27–24:53, NL; Jon. 3:1–21:25, NL
11 Smith, Marsha A. Ellis (Editor). *Holman Book of Biblical Charts.* (1984) page 35
12 Dake Bible, OT page 511, col. 1 "Apocryphal Books"
13 Dake Bible, OT page 877, col. 1 note to Dan. 8:20

Abbreviations

DK Dake Bible, Dake Publishing, Lawrenceville, GA
NL New Living Study Bible, Tyndale House Publishers, Wheaton, IL
NT New Testament
OT Old Testament

Chapter 13

The Millennium of Progress

T HE MILLENNIUM of A.D. 1000–2000 opens on the sour note
of the Crusades. Originally and ostensibly an effort to pos-
itively propagate God's Word, these events soon became a
disgrace to all things godly. For all the wrong reasons many were
hurt and relations between Muslims, Catholics, Hebrews, and
Christians – all believers at some level in the same Bible – suffered greatly. Many Bible-based religions lived the hypocrisy that
we now find very common. Unfortunately, this situation has not
improved much with age. God in Heaven must sorrow at the failure of those of mankind who deceptively identify themselves with
Him. He made it so simple for us to understand Him, but in our
selfish efforts many have lost an understanding and perspective
of Him.

In the 1300s Marco Polo made his journeys. Gunpowder was
invented and perfected in Europe. Wycliffe, Hus, and others
evolved their interpretations of the Bible. The Muslim (Islam)
Ottoman Empire came into being in Turkey and the Middle East.
Columbus "discovered" the Americas. Gutenberg invented the
printing press and the modern media business was born. And
finally, by 1500, Michelangelo painted and the "Protestant" Reformation was initiated under Luther, Calvin, and others.

Pascal discovered modern probability-inference theory. His
discoveries beg a very significant conclusion relative to biblical
prophecy. Probability inference predicts the outcome of future
events based on past events. Without getting into Pascal's mathematical theories in detail, simple intuition tells us that if over 50

percent of the events out of a population of six thousand predicted events occur perfectly over the course of many years, the likelihood of the other predicted events happening perfectly also is quite high.[1] Mathematically, it is actually astronomically high. The mathematical performance of biblical prophecy makes it impossible to rationally deny its future end-time predictions, which rapidly approach us.

We can be very sure that the remainder of biblical prophecy will happen someday, but when? The Bible tells us that no one knows the dates of certain final events except God, but we are given many clues regarding conditions on earth that will occur just before the Messiah returns.[2] These clues are outlined in the New Testament and must be thoughtfully understood in detail and in context with other relevant portions of the Bible.[3] A careful perusal of these chapters is convincing regarding near-term end-times events.

During this century Peter the Great ruled in Russia, Napoleon was in France, and the United States were born. Soon we had the automobile, the typewriter, and the telephone, followed by the airplane and computers.

World War I, World War II, and the atomic bomb caused all to comprehend, perhaps for the first time, the opportunity mankind has to totally annihilate itself. The armament that has occurred subsequently would lead most rational thinkers to conclude that it is only a matter of time before someone, either by accident or intent, accomplishes just that. However, God has another plan.

During all of this, God's people, the Hebrews, continued to be tortured and dispersed. Under severe duress, they began to be reunited in significant numbers in 1948 at the new National Home in Israel. As the historical literature conclusively proves, God performed a miracle, a miracle strongly opposed by Satan and His forces of darkness, in order for the new Israel to be established and continue.[4] Oh, what punishment the Hebrews have undergone for having, in their stiff-necked way, failed to listen to the repeated offers of God.

This second regathering is the principal proof that the clock for the end-times has truly finally started.[5]

The importance of the second regathering cannot be overexaggerated. God promised two dispersions of Israel due to their failure to keep the conditions of His covenants.

Many contract promises of a very final consequence for our covenant period engaged at the moment the renewed Israel took root. While few recognize the significance of this event, the outcomes are clearly detailed in Scripture and they are irreversible. The only matter of uncertainty (to us, not God) is the exact timing.[6]

At the conclusion of these events, the Hebrew remnant will once again return to God and His son, the Messiah.[7] The Messiah is conclusively Yeshua, or as many know Him, Jesus. That remnant will then become disciples and will evangelize the world for Him.[8]

We are now on the threshold of the new millennium, a time of increased pace and knowledge, and almost certainly a time for the final reckoning of God with rebellious people of any or no religious persuasion. After a long and patient wait, this reckoning will be the time of conclusion for Him. None who are serious about Him and accept His conditions will be left behind. Those who choose to acknowledge Him will survive. Those who choose not to acknowledge Him (with the exception of some who will go into the next millennium of the Messiah as "natural" people) will die and go to Hell where they will suffer incomprehensibly and continuously forever.[9] The choice between which of these two mutually exclusive paths is, and always has been, ours individually to make.

Chart 7

A.D. 1000	A.D. 1500	A.D. 2000

RENAISSANCE

MODERN AGE

Crusades

Marco Polo

Gun power – Europe
Wycliffe, Hus
Ottoman Empire (Muslim)
Printing
Columbus
Reformation
– Luther
– Calvin
Michelangelo

Pascal – Probability-inference theory
Peter the Great
Napolean

U.S. independence
Automobile
Typewriter
Telephone
Airplanes
Israel – Regathering
Computers
W.W. I
W.W. II

COVENANT PERIOD:
COVENANT OF GRACE (cont.)

TIMES OF THE GENTILES:
WORLD

ISRAELI RULE:
GENTILE

Notes, Chapter 13

1   Dake Bible, OT page 731, col 4 "Law of Compound Probability"; Dake Bible, NT page 241, col. 3 "20 Proofs Bible is Inspired" #12

2   Matt. 24:36, NL

3   Matt. 24:1–25:46, DK; Mark 13:1–37, DK

4   Thoene, Bodie. *The Zion Covenant and The Zion Chronicles.* (Series published 1986–91)

5   Isa. 11:11, DK

6   Matt. 24:36, DK

7   Zech. 13:8–9, DK

8   Dake Bible; NT page 311, col. 4 note 28

9   Zech. 14:16, DK

Abbreviations

DK   Dake Bible, Dake Publishing, Lawrenceville, GA

NL   New Living Study Bible, Tyndale House Publishers, Wheaton, IL

NT   New Testament

OT   Old Testament

Chapter 14

The Future

THE MOST SIGNIFICANT end-times personalities operating in a manner contrary to God's goal of a heavenly destiny for all of mankind are the Antichrist and the False Prophet. Their goal is to defeat God on behalf of Satan.[1] Many believe that the Antichrist may be alive right now.

The Antichrist

The Antichrist is a political leader who will rise to power out of a small country located inside the borders of the former Roman Empire. His initial headquarters will be in reconstructed Babylon, making it likely that he will originate from either Iraq or Syria. The former Roman Empire includes all of the countries immediately surrounding the Mediterranean going as far north as England and as far east as modern Iraq.[2]

The Antichrist will spring from his small, single-country base to subdue three other nations within this geography. Then, six other Roman Empire countries will submit to him.[3] He will subsequently go on to acquire countries to the east of the former Roman Empire that had been a part of the Grecian Empire (present-day Afghanistan, Bangladesh, Burma, India, Iran, Pakistan, parts of the former U.S.S.R., etc). In total, these areas represent roughly one-third of the world's population and one-third of the inhabitable land area.

He will be very articulate, generous, and compelling, and he will hate believers in God and even unbelieving Hebrews. Satan will grant him awesome supernatural powers, which he will use in his attempt to gain world rulership.[4]

The False Prophet

Assisting the Antichrist will be a world religious leader. The Bible calls this person the False Prophet.[5] The False Prophet will raise support from certain organized religions for the Antichrist. The False Prophet and the Antichrist will initially be partners. Halfway through the seven-year tribulation period, known as the end-times or Daniel's Seventieth Week, the Antichrist will demand to be worshiped as god, and the relationship with the False Prophet's cult will be broken.

A Preview

In business, we are told that effective communication requires major points to be made three times. I offer this preview as the first, followed by more detailed proofs, and then a summary.

The Bible foretells future events, but few of us relate biblical predictive elements to our day-to-day lives during this time of great comfort for many in the world. We intuitively assume that Bible prophecy applies primarily to the past.

As previously mentioned, of the over six thousand prophecies in the Bible, more than 50 percent have already been perfectly fulfilled.[6] A very few of the remaining need to occur for the time clock of Daniel's Seventieth Week to commence and the Messiah to come the second and final time.[7]

I believe that it is likely that we are living just prior to the era referred to in the Bible as the end-times.[8] These are the times just prior to the close of this covenant, the Covenant Period of Grace.

The remaining 40-plus percent of unfulfilled prophecies apply to a number of major events, including:

- the appearance of the Middle East–based dictator (called the Antichrist) who takes over three nations
- the signing of a seven-year peace pact between the nation of Israel and the Antichrist
- the rising of the powerful spiritual leader who will support the Antichrist. These two will lead military, commerce, and religion in the old Roman and Grecian Empire territories, initially out of Babylon (Iraq)
- the reestablishment of Hebrew temple worship and sacrifices on Temple Mount in Jerusalem
- the breach of the seven-year peace pact by the Antichrist and the profaning of the Hebrew sacrificial altar at the temple at the midpoint of the period
- the commencement of the Great Tribulation, a time of great trouble for Hebrews and the godly alike, initiated by Satan via his earthly servant the Antichrist[9]

Great Tribulation

The tribulation is a seven-year period of trauma predicted in Daniel that occurs just before the end of the present Covenant period.[10] It is commonly called Daniel's Seventieth Week.

The tribulation commences with the signing of the seven-year peace pact between Israel and the Antichrist. The Great Tribulation is the latter three and one-half years of the tribulation period. The midpoint is marked by the sacrifice of an unclean animal by the Antichrist on the Hebrew altar on Temple Mount in Jerusalem. At that time the Antichrist will also break his seven-year peace pact with Israel and demand worship by all of his subjects. During the Great Tribulation, life for the Hebrews will be worse than at any previous time in history.[11] This is called the

"Time of Jacob's Trouble" in Scripture.[12] Millions of Hebrews and Gentiles will perish.[13]

God will permit the tribulation to separate those who really follow Him from the phonies. This will include a cleansing of both Israel and those who claim membership in His church. There will be an Israeli remnant who come to repentance as they realize that the Messiah is Yeshua.[14]

No one knows for certain whether the tribulation will affect nations outside the territory of the old Roman and Greek Empires.[15] It is my opinion that only the old Roman and Grecian territories will be directly affected. Certainly, however, military forces from all over the world will be involved, bringing about a high level of impact upon every nation.[16]

The following events will commence at the middle of the Seventieth Week, three and one-half years prior to the final battle of Armageddon:

- the movement of the world headquarters of the Antichrist to Jerusalem
- the Sign in the Sky announcing the commencement of God's wrath
- the most likely time for the bodily resurrection and rapture of believers to meet the Messiah in the sky
- the requirement for a mark of identification on the body for trading in the empire of the Antichrist
- the commencement of the judgment and rewards of God's raptured followers in Heaven
- the movement from Heaven to earth of the battle between God and Satan for the spirits of mankind[17]

At the end of this seven-year period God will judge the nations for their behavior toward Israel.[18]

Millennium

This thousand-year period of peace on earth commences just after the defeat of the Antichrist at the battle of Armageddon. It will be during this period that the Messiah, returning as the King of the earth, will provide the world an opportunity to live free of spiritual rebellion.[19]

This will initiate a time of universal peace and prosperity. Sickness, calamities, wars, and other negative aspects of life will disappear.

Man will still retain a depraved nature during the millennium but with no Satanic influence, opportunities for overcoming tendencies toward natural sin will be greater than during the present covenant period. However, many individuals will still rebel at the end of the thousand years.[20] They will have a choice to follow God after living under evil-free Messianic leadership for up to one thousand years. Many will not choose to follow God and will be lost. After the close of this millennium, those who choose God will commence the repopulation of earth. This period has been predicted in the Old Testament many times.[21]

Natural people alive at the end of Armageddon and those born after the millennium commences will enjoy long life (except for death penalty sinners).

After a final purging at the end of the millennium, there will be no return to failure in the future. Evil will be destroyed permanently.[22] Events prophesied to follow the millennium include:

- the release of Satan for a short period to collect remaining evil people on earth, after which they will be summarily disposed of by God
- the final and permanent consignment of Satan and the rest of the wicked to Hell
- the bodily resurrection, judgment, and permanent consignment to Hell of the wicked dead
- the cleansing renovation of the earth by fire

- the descent of the holy city of Jerusalem from Heaven to earth
- the eternal future with God, the Messiah, and the Holy spirit reigning from the new Jerusalem[23]

These things may seem far-fetched, but then again, so did the breakup of the U.S.S.R. a few years ago and the reestablishment of Israel and the Hebrew language after over nineteen hundred years of dispersion.

The Detail

Daniel's Seventieth Week, Matthew 24, and John's Revelation are the key areas of prophecy that must be studied carefully in order to understand end-times events.

As in any discussion of future events, the facts are buried under a pile of opinions, which must be sorted through. The Messiah tells us specifically that no one except God knows the exact timing of these final future events. Therefore, some speculation is included in this book as it is in all similar works.[24]

However, the Bible does provide us with clues in abundance, many "signs" to look for, and much information from which to draw educated conclusions about events and situations that must be in place for the end-times to commence. My attempt will be to take a rational, straightforward, unstrained look at the evidence we have and offer what seems logical and fits the criteria of being biblically harmonious. We will depend on the Bible to interpret itself wherever possible and assume that everything that can be interpreted literally should receive that treatment.

My conclusions will be in some conflict with those of some scholars and writers. I respect them and their opinions. Some of their interpretations will be pointed out as appropriate. References will be made to other materials so that you can check these matters out and reach your own conclusions.

All that said, I humbly offer up the following for your consideration.

What are the conditions required for these end-times to commence? Could Daniel's Seventieth Week be upon us very early in this millennium, maybe even early in the twenty-first century? The principal proof that these events are underway now, and not previously, is that the second and final regathering of Israel promised in the Bible has started. The Hebrews *must* reside in Israel for remaining prophecies to become feasible. All remaining items of unfulfilled prophesy can now fit rationally into the promised end-times and they can come quickly.

I believe that we are arguably in a time when Daniel's Seventieth Week, the seven-year period preceding the end of life as we know it, will soon be upon us. This is not to say that life on earth will cease. After severe trauma, life will go on but under very different circumstances and for a much smaller number of people.

It appears that there are only a few notable events that must yet occur before we need to presume that we are at the doorstep of the Seventieth Week.

Babylon

First, the city of Babylon must be developing into a significant commercial center in order for it to be destroyed as predicted.[25] Today, in 2000, over one million people live in the area of the old city of Babylon. The largest nearby development today is the city of Hillah.

The War of Ezekiel

Second, it seems likely to me that the war described in Ezekiel 38 and 39 must occur prior to the commencement of the Seventieth Week. It should be noted that many scholars conclude that the events of Ezekiel occur at the end of the Seventieth Week in conjunction with the battle of Armageddon, rather than before it as I am proposing. However, it seems both feasible and logical that these Ezekiel events are likely to occur before the Seventieth Week even gets started.

For one thing, the physiological events are different between the Seventieth Week battle of Armageddon and the battle of Ezekiel. The following matrix of cosmic occurrences summarizes the differences between the events of Ezekiel, Matthew, and Revelation. Based upon other factors, it is clear that Matthew and Revelation without question apply to the time of Armageddon.

	Ezekiel	Matthew 24	Revelation 6
Overflowing rain	✓		
Hailstones	✓		
Fire and brimstone	✓		
Sun darkened		✓	✓
Moon darkened		✓	✓
Stars fall		✓	✓
Heaven shaken/departed		✓	✓

In Ezekiel 38:1–7 the prediction is made that nations from the area of southern Russia, Northern Europe, Armenia, Iran, Ethiopia, and Libya will make war on Israel. These nations do not include a major portion of the Antichrist's territory that we know is assembled for Armageddon.

Also, the argument that Ezekiel's war is started at the end of Daniel's Seventieth Week by the forces conquered by the Antichrist during his battles to the north and east does not seem supportable because the Antichrist is not clearly mentioned in these Ezekiel verses.

Evaluating word patterns is an accepted method of determining the periodicity of a biblical phrase by studying it in context wherever it is used in the Bible. This methodology results in associating events with a common or near-common timing. A study of all scriptural occurrences of the phrases "after many days" and "in the latter years," which are the phrases used in the book of Ezekiel, does not lead us to the conclusion that these phrases are associated with the end of the Seventieth Week. Only expressions such as latter day(s), last day(s), and last time(s) clearly apply to Armageddon. These phrases are not found in Ezekiel.

These Ezekiel events occur after the second and final regathering, but when Israel is at peace (Ezekiel 38:8–11). This period of peace cannot be the same as Armageddon because the Antichrist will have broken the peace pact with Israel three and one-half years earlier and established military control over the country. That period will not be a period of peace in Israel.

God uses the personal pronoun I over twenty times in these two chapters of Ezekiel. It is clear that He is referring to Himself, not His Son, the Messiah. Yet the primary divine personality at the battle of Armageddon is definitely the Messiah.[26] I conclude that these two different members of the Trinity are involved in two different events.

Other evidence supporting a pre–Seventieth Week timing for the events of Ezekiel is the description of a period of over seven months for the burial of the bones of those killed in this war. Burial will probably not even be feasible following Armageddon due to the massive geophysical changes predicted.[27]

To further validate this possibility, in Ezekiel 39 we see a seven-year period following this conflict in which the Israelis consume no fuel except that left over from the attack. This fuel must come from the military apparatus left by the enemy when they are defeated by God. Why would this source of fuel (and weaponry) be necessary if the Messiah has returned, restored their land, and restored Israel to power?[28]

Compellingly, this seven-year supply of fuel and weapons also lines up nicely with the period of Daniel's Seventieth Week, which commences with three and one-half years of peace for Israel. It seems logical because the outcome discussed in Ezekiel would put Israel in a position of great military strength and negotiating power. Their natural (Arab) enemies would be in a weakened position. Israel would be miraculously (supernaturally) strong. Israel could demand peace, and the right to erect a temple (perhaps prefabricated) so that daily sacrificial practices could be reinstituted for the first time since A.D. 70.

Certainly, if the past is any predictor of the future, world powers will have a propensity to support the wishes of the Arab nations because they will not be anxious to aggravate the oil-rich Arab leaders. The latter will be particularly reluctant to include Temple Mount privileges to Israel. So it is unlikely that Israel will get this prophesied privilege without being in a position of great strength.

It is more rational that peace and temple worship would come if Israel were in a powerful position to negotiate, as it will be after the Ezekiel war. Based on the above, it would appear that Ezekiel's war will occur just prior to the commencement of the Seventieth Week.

The only logical conclusion is that Ezekiel must apply to another (earlier, since there is no later) period.

Seven-Year Peace Pact

A third event that must occur before the Seventieth Week can begin is the signing of the seven-year peace pact between Israel and its Arab neighbors.[29] While it would appear that this pact could come about almost any day (since we constantly read about Middle East peace in the newspapers), certain characteristics that must be a part of this particular peace pact are not evident in bargains presently under consideration.

These neighbors must include the head of a small nation, probably present-day Syria or Iraq. This leader, the Antichrist, is described identically in Daniel and Revelation. He will rapidly subdue three surrounding nations. Following that, six other

Roman Empire territory countries will submit voluntarily to him.[30]

There is a great deal of evidence to support that this person will come from the territory of the old nation of Syria, which includes present-day Syria, part of Iran, and Iraq.[31] It would be pragmatic to conclude that the three small nations he will subdue will be Egypt, Greece, and Turkey, or at least nations in the immediate area of Syria and Israel. Once these three nations are subdued by him, the six other old Roman Empire nations will agree to his leadership (possibilities here include nations like Romania, Italy, Germany, England, France, and Spain) and his quest for world dictatorship will be underway.

We should keep in mind that this seven-year triggering agreement could be private or public. World citizenry may or may not be aware when this contract is signed.

Valley of Jehoshaphat

We must now take a somewhat brief diversion, not really necessary to get where we are going, but rather for completeness. This diversion addresses what I conclude to be an unrelated matter that is sometimes also confused with the Seventieth Week. I am speaking of the Valley of Jehoshaphat event. Upon study, I believe that it can be rationally concluded that this event probably precedes even our present times and, certainly, the Seventieth Week.

In the book of Joel, early in Chapter 3, we read of a time future to Joel associated with the second regathering of the Hebrews back to Israel. During this second regathering, a meeting of the nations is spoken of. This meeting is to occur in the "Valley of Jehoshaphat."

The Bible doesn't tell us specifically where the Valley of Jehoshaphat is, but the only valley of consequence related to King Jehoshaphat seems to be the one in the Negev desert of Israel, probably east of the present city of Gaza. That is where God miraculously filled trenches with water for a military campaign involving Jehoshaphat and others he was in league with.[32]

In Joel 3 we read that God will "gather all nations and bring them down to the Valley of Jehoshaphat" in these "latter days" (not the day of the Lord, or Armageddon). It turns out there was a meeting in February of 1937 in Nahal which is also just east of Gaza. At that meeting inquiries regarding the destiny of Palestine as a home for the Hebrews were held. This meeting included the Arab nations. At that meeting, the future of Israel was pled for passionately by Chaim Weizmann, whom most consider to be one of the fathers of modern Israel. Perhaps this event fulfills this prediction and Weizmann was God's agent at that moment, or perhaps it was another early event.[33] In any case, it seems logical to conclude that the events predicted early in Joel are likely to have occurred over sixty years ago.

Later, in Joel 3:14, we see the phrase "the day of the Lord." These late Joel 3 events obviously *do* apply to the later times of Armageddon.

The Seventieth Week

We are now ready to move sequentially on to the last seven years of the present covenant period, which will most likely commence when commercial status in Babylon, Ezekiel's war, and the peace pact have materialized. The first half of the Seventieth Week, known as the "beginning of sorrows," will find the Hebrews firmly entrenched in Israel, at peace, and enjoying temple worship on Temple Mount in Jerusalem in accordance with their tradition. This will include animal sacrifice for sin atonement, since the Hebrews still believe that this is necessary because they do not believe that the Messiah has come yet. All of the necessary implements for this worship, including the proper "red heifer," are available now for the first time in centuries, awaiting the day when access to Temple Mount is achieved. We know that the

Antichrist's conquests of the six Roman Empire nations will also be underway during this time. Peace between the Antichrist and Israel will facilitate these early conquests.

The Judgements

In a study of this crucial period, interest inevitably and quickly focuses on the timing of the judgement events revealed in the book of Revelation, rather than the validity of the events themselves. Almost everyone who gets this far does not question the probability of the events occurring; they are accepted.

The order of these events is tied to a sequential timing scheme. These judgements come in groups of seven and are metaphorically referred to in the Bible in a specific order starting with the seven seals, followed by the seven trumpets (which have embedded in them the seven thunders), which are followed finally by the seven vials (sometimes referred to as bowls). This presentation of judgements is discussed in Revelation, chapters 6–18.

Seals were the method used in the days of John, the recorder of Revelation, to provide confidentiality and authentication for documents. A seal certified that a document was sent by a certain person and/or that the document was to be opened only by a certain person. In the case of Revelation, there are seven seals covering the trailing edge of a scroll. All of these seals must be opened mechanically and in sequence before the other judgements can be understood and come into effect. The Messiah is the only one qualified to open these seals.[34]

It is likely that the first seal occurs just after the Week commences.[35] It is almost universally understood to represent the coming of the Antichrist, Satan's end-times senior agent on earth. The Antichrist is represented in the vision of John, the scribe for Revelation, by the metaphor of a white horse. The color white would normally be associated with the Messiah, which illustrates the common practice of counterfeiting from the evil side. He is a counterfeit Christ.

The second seal clearly represents the wars in the old Roman and Grecian Empire territories that the Antichrist will undertake in his quest for world domination.[36]

The third seal represents famine and plagues.[37] There is some suggestion that the Antichrist will hoard food so that he can gain more control over the nations he seeks to dominate.

The fourth seal represents the widespread death of many that follows war, famine, and plagues.[38] The portion of the earth affected in all of these matters is in dispute. It could be anywhere from one-fourth of the combined territories of the Roman and Grecian Empires to one-fourth of the total earth.[39] I believe that the strongest support for a limited definition of the land area is the fact that the Bible uses another phrase when it means the entire world. That phrase is "under the whole heaven." This latter phrase is employed eight times in Scripture from Genesis through Daniel and clearly is used when God has the entire world in view.[40]

In further support of this position, in a Revelation Scripture referring to the scope of the Antichrist's control, the word "power" would be more correctly translated "influence."[41] Certainly it would be correct to expect that these Middle Eastern, European, and Asian events would have a major "influence" on "total world" affairs. I therefore conclude that when the term "earth" is used in end-times discussions, the land area is limited to the old Roman and Grecian territories.

The focus of the fifth seal shifts from earth to Heaven and reveals there a scene in which martyrs previously slain for the cause of God cry out to Him for judgement.[42] They are given white robes and told to wait for a short time for God to undertake vengeance on their behalf.

It should be noted that we have no definite timing information on these seal judgements, except that they must commence after the peace pact is signed and are certainly completed prior to the Sixth Seal. It is possible that they may be experienced over equal time periods, but probably not.

Sixth Seal

The Sixth Seal is a point of strong definition for the end-times. It is a direct response to the disciples' inquiry of the Messiah, reported early in Matthew 24, requesting a "sign" for end-time events.

A logical place to begin trying to understand the timing of the Sixth Seal is to account for everything with a firm, provable date first, and then to put other events into proper sequence with relation to the events having definite timing.

The following events all occur during the last half of Daniel's Seventieth Week, a period of three and one-half years, or forty-two months, prior to Armageddon:

- the saints of the most High ... will be given into the Antichrist's hand for exactly forty-two months to be severely tested, while he will also think to change the times and the laws
- the power of the Israelis will be scattered for exactly forty-two months (This further supports my Ezekiel interpretation, because the Israelis must have power in order for that power to be scattered.)
- the Gentiles (i.e. the Antichrist) will control Jerusalem (but not necessarily the temple) for exactly forty-two months
- the two witnesses (probably Enoch and Elijah) will be sent to earth to represent God on earth for exactly forty-two months
- Hebrews will flee from the Antichrist into the wilderness for exactly forty-two months. The Hebrews will be

nourished during their forty-two-month flight from
Satan
- Satan's earthly leader, the Antichrist, is given exactly
forty-two months from the midpoint of the Week to
remain in power
- Satan will be cast from Heaven to earth and he will per-
secute the Hebrews and believers for exactly forty-two
months[43]

The last of these events, the casting of Satan from Heaven to
earth, occurs at the seventh, or last, trumpet. That means that
since the seal judgements precede the trumpet judgements, and
for the mechanical reasons explained before, both of these two
categories of judgements must be completed by the middle of
the Seventieth Week. (That leaves only the vial judgements to
occur after the middle of the Week.)

We have therefore pinpointed the final Trumpet judgement
event at the midpoint of Daniel's Seventieth Week. If we can pin-
point the earliest judgement event of the midpoint, everything
else must occur in-between.

The Wrath of God

The Bible talks about two major categories of wrath during the
end-times. The first is the period of the wrath of God, which
commences at the Sixth Seal.[44] The second is the wrath of Satan,
which commences with the seventh trumpet.[45]

The wrath of Satan, as we have seen above, commences forty-
two months prior to Armageddon at mid-Week. It is logical that
God would move His wrath to earth at the very same time Satan
moves his wrath as he is cast from Heaven. Would God take a
hiatus in battle for a period of time for some reason? A time-out?
I don't believe that this is just a fun spectator sport with those

kinds of rules. There is every indication that Satan will not be taking a break, so how could God?

The logical conclusion, then, is that the combative, super-power wrath of both of these spirit powers moves simultaneously from Heaven to earth, with only three and one-half years to play out the event.

Clearly, God promises to protect believing mankind from this battle between God and Satan on earth.[46] However, do these promises exclude believing mankind from the activities of the first five seals which occur during the earlier parts of the Seventieth Week? I don't think so. All of the disciples and apostles suffered, so why should this generation of believers be excluded? The only promise made, and that very specifically, is that believers would escape the wrath, not the events leading up to the wrath.

So the important question is the timing of the Sixth Seal.

A logical conclusion is that the Sixth Seal, representing the commencement of God's wrath, and the Seventh Trumpet, representing the commencement of Satan's wrath, occur at about the same time, on the same day, at the midpoint of the Week.

In summary, we know that God's wrath starts just after the Sixth Seal because the Word of God tells us so.[47] Because His wrath also starts with the first vial, and also must start when Satan's wrath moves to earth, all of the events between the Sixth Seal and the first vial must occur on the same day, at the midpoint of Daniel's Seventieth Week. It will be a very busy day.

Raptures

Raptures are events that involve the disappearance of those who believe or have believed to God's domain in Heaven, where they will ultimately live peacefully and trouble-free. A rapture can occur before or after bodily death. The major rapture coming soon that concerns most knowledgeable believers includes those who truly believe in God who have previously died since the first visit of the Messiah, as well as believers who are now alive.[48] Both groups of these believers will be transported to Heaven for judgment, rewards, and future assignments.[49]

For completeness, the Bible presents us with several raptures:

- the rapture of Enoch (predeath)
- the rapture of Elijah (predeath)
- the rapture of the Messiah and the Old Testament saints
- the rapture of the saints (the large, partially predeath rapture in question here). Note: I refer to this as the believer rapture
- the rapture of the 144,000 Hebrew "elect" of Revelation(future)
- the rapture of the two witnesses of Revelation (future)
- the rapture of the tribulation saints at the end of this age (future)[50]

The timing of the believer rapture is a key subject of much importance and dispute among believers. Many believers assume that they will be raptured prior to any events of the Seventieth Week. Other believers expect to live through all of the end-time events.

It appears most consistent with Scripture that the believer rapture will occur as predicted in Matthew 24 and Revelation 6, at the opening of the Sixth Seal, which must fall at the midpoint of the Seventieth Week in order for other Scripture to match without tension. The Sixth Seal occurs just after the abomination of desolation when the Antichrist desecrates a swine on the Hebrew altar.[51] This is after Jerusalem has been encompassed by Antichrist.[52]

Some challenge this position based on the belief that the believer rapture cannot occur until the gospel has been preached to all the world, and offer this as a reason why the believer rapture cannot come.[53] However, many scholars believe this coverage has already been accomplished, as the territory in view here is commonly interpreted as either the "civilized" world or, alternatively, only the old Holy Roman Empire territory. Both have certainly been more than adequately served already.

However, all of that said, it is dangerous to speculate on this issue. If we choose to believe in a believer rapture before the tribulation events, as many do, and it does not occur according to our expectations, believers may lose faith as a consequence of being unprepared for a later believer rapture. If we expect a later believer rapture and it comes early, we may have convinced ourselves to put off a commitment decision until we see the predicted events begin to occur, and by then it will be too late. The Messiah tells us not to worry, that His Father will take care of us, just to be prepared at any time. I believe that is the best advice.

Day of the Lord

To avoid any further confusion on this matter, we must also clear up the meaning of the phrase "day of the Lord" (as contrasted with "day of the Lord's wrath"). This phrase, including the plural form, occurs in twenty-eight Scriptures. It is clear that this is a period that commences with the day of the battle of Armageddon at the end of the Seventieth Week and not at the midpoint. Several Scriptures make this clear:

- the dividing of spoils of a war (Armageddon)
- geophysical conditions of a different sort than those of Matthew 24 and Revelation 6
- the melting of the elements, which occurs at the end of the millennium
- destruction of the wicked, which occurs at the end of the millennium[54]

This should prove that the day of the Lord is not the same as the time of the Sixth Seal, the latter of which is the commencement of the wrath of God.

It is also very important to remember that as shown, the believer rapture is at a different time than Armageddon. The believer rapture will come first, at the midpoint, and the Messiah apparently will not come all the way to earth. He will meet the saints in the air. Three and one-half years later, the Messiah will return all the way to the earth for the battle of Armageddon.[55]

In summary, the somewhat uncomfortable, but apparently logical, conclusion must be that all of the events between the Sixth Seal and the first vial, including the believer rapture, happen at the same time, at the mid-Week point, three and one-half years after the signing of the peace pact and three and one-half years before Armageddon.

Other Mid-Week Events

There are some other less argumentative mid-Week events that should be mentioned, more for awareness than for supporting the previous discussion of the timing of events.

God's two witnesses, most likely Enoch and Elijah, will arrive on earth and take over from the "hinderer" of lawlessness (probably the true church) as the latter departs the earth in rapture. The primary argument that the church is the hinderer is that masculine pronouns are commonly used when referring to the church, and that the hinderer is "taken," as in rapture.[56]

The 144,000 Hebrew evangelists are sealed, or marked for divine protection, from the judgements that are coming next to earth. Many of the other Hebrews (the remnant) flee Jerusalem for the protection of the surrounding wilderness, mostly to western Jordan (see Petra below). The ground will swallow up the forces of the Antichrist as they pursue the remnant in flight.[57]

The judgement of the locusts and the slaying of one-third of mankind (most likely only those within the old Roman and Grecian Empires) will occur at mid-Week also.[58]

Petra

Petra, called Sela and Bozrah in Scripture, is a huge natural fortress a few hours southeast of Jerusalem that is reserved for the Hebrews when they flee from the Antichrist after he breaks his peace covenant with Israel at the midpoint of the tribulation.[59] I have seen it personally and it is unique and awesome.

It is located in southwestern Jordan, and is a huge area capable of protecting many thousands of people. Virtually impregnable by land, it has only one decent land approach through a mile-long crevice several stories high. It also contains several water springs which will be obviously necessary for survival.

The Israeli remnant will be safe there because the Antichrist will be challenged by countries from the north and the east early during the second half of the Week, and he will be forced to depart Israel with most of his military apparatus in order to maintain control over the territory he has already conquered. This will result in a "shortening" of the persecution by Satan's agents of those gentile and Jewish persons who have come to a belief in God as a result of witnessing the mid-Week events.[60] Still, apparently two-thirds of all Israel will not make it through the Seventieth Week alive; many believers will be lost as well.[61]

Also, it would seem that shortly after mid-Week the 144,000 Hebrew evangelists will be raptured to Heaven. This seems unusual, because they were just protected (sealed). These evangelists will come back later, after the battle of Armageddon is won.[62]

The earth will experience the wrath of Satan and the awesome power of God and the Messiah as the battle for the destiny of the spirits of remaining mankind gets underway here on earth. Both Hebrews and new believers are in for a time of punishment by Satan and his forces as has never before been experienced on earth. Multitudes will be destroyed. God's purpose in permitting these events will be to purify Israel and those who become believers.[63]

Satan will employ all of his demon powers, which will be so awesome that they will confuse even those who have come to accept God and His conditions after understanding the implications of the midpoint believer rapture that has just occurred.[64]

God's two witnesses will teach the truth, assist the believers and the Hebrews, and have more supernatural power at their disposal than any of Satan's forces until the final three and one-half years are over.[65]

The Antichrist will require forced worship of himself as supreme deity within the nations he controls. He will require a mark of some kind on the body of each individual in the territory. (This could be in the form of a tattoo or a microchip.) Those who believe in God are commanded to avoid taking this "mark of the beast" or they will lose their possibility for a heavenly afterlife.[66]

The Vial Judgements

The vial judgements will commence as the period of God and Satan's wrath gets underway. It is logical that at least the last of these judgements would begin just prior to the battle of Armageddon. Certainly the vial judgements will "soften up" the Antichrist's forces. These vials contain plagues and are directed at those who have taken the mark of the Antichrist. They are described as follows:

- the first vial will result in awful sores on those with the mark and those who have worshipped the Antichrist
- the second vial will pollute the sea, probably just the Mediterranean but perhaps more broadly
- the third vial will similarly pollute the rivers and water sources
- the fourth will increase the power of the sun, scorching mankind
- the fifth will cause darkness on earth[67]

Other Related Events

In Daniel, a period of daily sacrifice followed by the desecration of the temple is described as lasting 2300 days.[68] Since we know that the period of daily sacrifice is forty-two months (the first half of the Seventieth Week) and that the temple is then desecrated, we can subtract 1260 days (forty-two months times thirty days) from the 2300, leaving 1040 days.

These 1040 days then must pass during the initial part of the second half of Daniel's Seventieth Week until the "sanctuary is cleansed." A cleansing will require the Hebrews to forcibly take back the temple at that point, even though they will not conquer the city.

Dividing these 1040 days into months shows that they will be thirty-four months and 20 days into the second half of the Week by the time the Hebrews cleanse the temple and reestablish temple worship for the second time.

Subtracting 1040 days from 1260, we would conclude that the Hebrew reestablishment of temple worship will occur seven months and ten days prior to Armageddon, the latter of which occurs at the end of the seven years. The two witnesses will probably assist them in the recapture of the temple.

We know that the Hebrews do not necessarily recapture all of Jerusalem, probably just the temple.[69]

During these times, many will come to an understanding of God.[70] For them, and all others who come to God during this last three-and-one-half-year period and live through it, there will be a final rapture of the "tribulation saints," just prior to Armageddon.[71]

As things are resolved favorably for the Antichrist to the north and the east, he will return to Israel just before the close of the Seventieth Week with his armies to destroy all Hebrews once and for all. He will be joined by his new allies from the north and the east.[72]

The sixth vial will dry up the river Euphrates so that these easterly armies can enter Israel. At this point all of the Antichrist's evil will be collected in one place for the battle of Armageddon. The result will be the destruction of the Antichrist.[73]

The final judgement vial will come in conjunction with Armageddon. The seventh vial will bring unbelievable thunder, lightning, great hail, and an earthquake to Babylon (which will be utterly destroyed), Jerusalem, and other great cities.[74] At this point, God is ready for the battle of Armageddon to be fought.

Even after all of the devastating problems and massive displays of God's power, Satan and the Antichrist will not give up. They will still want to fight the battle of Armageddon in a desperate hope for victory. The battle will get underway in the valley of Meggido about an hour north of Jerusalem. There the Messiah and His supernatural army will engage their enemy in battle for the final time in a one-day fight when much evil will be brought to its knees. God will assist the Messiah.[75]

The result will be the defeat of Satan by the Messiah and those who have willfully given themselves to Him. The latter will enjoy a life of harmony with Him and leadership assignments for Him forever. Universal religion will soon be established.[76]

After the battle of Armageddon is over, the ministry of the two witnesses will come to an end, and God will permit them to be killed by Satan's agents so that they too can become resurrected residents of Heaven, rather than going forth with the natural humans that remain.[77]

Once the two witnesses and the tribulation saints are raptured and believer judgement completed, the celebration of the victory of the Messiah will be held.[78]

The surviving one-third of the Hebrews will completely change their attitude about Yeshua and recognize Him as Messiah after their miraculous deliverance from certain death at the hands of the Antichrist.[79]

The Antichrist and his aide, the False Prophet, will be cast alive into the lake of fire, there to live forever in torment. Satan will be chained in the bottomless pit for one thousand years, then be released for another purpose.[80]

Finally, of great importance to the U.S. and other countries, will be the judgement of the nations, which will determine which nations will be permitted to enter the millennium based on their treatment of Israel.[81]

Other End-Times Periods

There are some other interesting end-time periods that bear some discussion. In Daniel 12:11, a period of 1290 days is presented following the mid-Week desolation rather than the conventional 1260 days, or forty-two months. Here we read that the "daily sacrifice will be taken away" 1290 days after the abomination is set up by the Antichrist. These extra thirty days, beyond the one-day battle of Armageddon, may refer to the time necessary for the Hebrews to discontinue temple sacrifice after they come to realize, under the ministry of the 144,000 Hebrew evangelists spoken of in Revelation, that animal sacrifice is no longer necessary, that the Messiah has come (again).

Daniel 12:12 refers to a 1335-day period following the mid-Week desolation. This verse perhaps refers to a special blessing for those "natural" humans who survive this trauma. Included in this trauma will be massive geophysical changes for seventy-five days after the battle of Armageddon.

Messiah's Government

The Messiah will establish His kingdom on earth following Armageddon and the geophysical changes which have taken place. The temple of Ezekiel 40–43 will be erected.

The Messiah's government, free of evil and political intrigue, will be established with King David at the head, while those raptured will serve as rulers and administrators in the universe. The surviving one-third of the Israelites, supported by the 144,000, will become the perpetual spiritual leaders after they gather in Jerusalem and acknowledge the Messiah. The veil between them and God will be lifted.[82]

Those natural non-Hebrew people left on earth will be able to live without the influence of evil for the first time since the sin of Adam and Eve in the Garden of Eden.[83] Life on earth will not, however, be without evil during this period. The lingering effect of Satan's earlier influence will continue until the end of the millennium.[84]

Israel's promised land grant, which has never been achieved, will be perfected, with one strip provided to each tribe.[85]

Preparation

I believe that the best way to prepare for these events is to be aware of them and to plan accordingly. Certainly there will be a time of severe trauma for believers when it may be difficult to survive without cooperating with the forces of the world dictator. Cooperation with the dictator will constitute a violation of the principals of belief in God, and will result in loss of eternal life in Heaven.[86]

Those with means are called to plan for these events now, prior to the believer rapture, by assigning worldly possessions upon death or rapture to trustworthy corporations or individuals not likely to be raptured, so that God's work has a means of continuance after the believer rapture.

We are called to understand the above and live accordingly, to be fully aware of the methods of the other side, and to cling to our hope and faith through these upcoming, horrendously difficult times.

Chart 8

A.D. 2000 | A.D. 2500 | A.D. 3000

MILLENNIUM

Satan chained
Messianic world rulership
Israel restored
Saints rule

70th Week of Daniel *

Ezekiel War

COVENANT PERIOD:
DIVINE GOVERNMENT

TIMES OF THE GENTILES:
ENDS FOREVER

ISRAELI RULE:
DIVINE

*see **Chart 9**, page 160

WATER   ROMAN   GRECIAN   ROMAN/GRECIAN OVERLAP

Chart 9 – Daniel's 70th Week

A.D. 2000		
YEAR 0	**3.5 YEARS**	**7 YEARS**
BEGINNING OF SORROWS	**GREAT TRIBULATION**	**MILLENNIUM**

BEGINNING OF SORROWS

7-year peace pact – Temple worship
1st Seal – Antichrist
2nd Seal – Wars
3rd Seal – Famine and plagues
4th Seal – Death
5th Seal – Heavenly martyrs

Conditions required for 70th week
• Babylon a budding commercial trade center
• War of Ezekiel 38–39 over
• 7-year peace pact

Midpoint*

GREAT TRIBULATION

Mark of the beast, forced worship
Rapture of 144,000
Vial (bowl) judgements
    1 – mankind
    2–5 – material

* Midpoint
Peace pact broken, sacrifice stopped
Antichrist conquers Israel, moves headquarters
6th Seal – Day of the Lord commences
    (earthquakes, sun darkened, stars fall, etc.)
2 witnesses arrive, church departs via believer rapture
144,000 sealed, remnant flees to wilderness
Trumpet judgements
    1–4 material
    5-6 mankind
    7 – Satan cast from Heaven, battle moves to earth

MILLENNIUM

Recapture of temple
6th Vial – Euphrates
2 witnesses raptured
Rapture – Trib. saints
Judgement of saved
7th Vial
Babylon falls
Armageddon
Antichrist and False Prophet in the lake of fire
Satan – bottomless pit
Messianic Government
Times of Gentiles over

Notes, Chapter 14

1 Dake Bible, OT pages 879–80, col. 2 "Antichrist, the King of the North"; Rev. 13:11–15, 19:20, DK

2 Dake Bible, chart 11

3 Dan. 7:23–25, DK; Dan. 11:40, DK; Rev. 17:12–17, DK

4 Dan. 11:36, DK; Rev. 13:1, DK; 2 Thess. 2: 8–10, DK; Rev. 13: 1–4, DK; Dake Bible, note 4 to Rev. 19:19

5 Rev. 13:11–15, 19:20, DK

6 Dake Bible, NT page 241, col. 3 note 12

7 Walvoord, John. *Every Prophecy of the Bible.* (1999)

8 Dake Bible, OT pages 877–880 col. 3 "The 70 Weeks"; NT page 308, col. 4 "31 Facts About Babylon"

9 Dan. 7:24, DK; Rev. 13, DK; Dan. 9:27, DK; Rev. 13:11–18, DK; Dan. 9:27, DK; Matt. 24:15, DK; Dan. 11:45–12:1, DK; Matt. 24:21, DK; Rev. 12–19, DK

10 Dake Bible, OT page 880, col. 2 "The Tribulation"; Dake Bible, OT page 53, col. 4 note 24

11 Dan. 9:27, DK; Dake Bible, OT page 877, col. 3 note 1.2; Rev. 11:2, DK

12 Jer. 30:7, DK

13 Zech. 13:8, DK; Rev. 6: 9–11, 7:9–17, DK

14 Zech. 14:16, DK

15 Dake Bible, NT page 308, col. 1 "Extent of Antichrist's Reign"

16 Dake Bible, OT page 880, col. 3 "Will the Tribulation be Worldwide?"; NT page 308, col. 1 "Extent of Antichrist's Reign"

Abbreviations

DK Dake Bible, Dake Publishing, Lawrenceville, GA
NL New Living Study Bible, Tyndale House Publishers, Wheaton, IL
NT New Testament
OT Old Testament

Notes, Chapter 14 (continued)

17 Dan. 11:45, DK; 2 Thess. 2:4, DK; Matt. 24:29, DK; 1 Thess. 4:16–17, DK; Rev. 13:16–17, 16:16, 19:19, 20:2, 20:4, DK; 1 Cor. 3:13–15, DK

18 Isa. 2:4, DK; Matt. 25:31–46, DK

19 Rev. 20:4, DK; Dake Bible, NT page 311, col. 3–4 "In Scripture it is Called"

20 Rev. 20:7–8, DK

21 Dake Bible, note to Pss. 72:2

22 Rev. 21: 4–7, DK

23 Rev. 20:7–15, 21:2, DK; 2 Pet. 3:7, 10–13, DK

24 Matt. 24:36, DK

25 Rev. 18, DK

26 Rev. 19: 11–21, DK

27 Rev. 16:18–20, DK

28 Zeph. 3:18–20, DK

29 Dan. 9:27, DK

30 Dake Bible, OT page 879, col. 2 "Antichrist, the King of the North"; Dan. 7: 8,24, DK; Rev. 17:13, DK

31 Dake Bible, NT page 309, col. 4 note 18; OT page 879, col. 3 "From Where Does Antichrist Come?"

32 1 Kings 3, DK

33 Sachar, Howard M. *A History of Israel.* (1996) page 203

34 Rev. 5:5–7, DK

35 Rev. 6:1–2, DK

36 Rev. 6:3–4, DK

37 Rev. 6:5–6, DK

38 Rev. 6:7–8, DK

39 Dake Bible, NT page 308, col. 1 "Extent of Antichrist's Reign"

40 Gen. 7:19, DKl; Deut. 2:25, 4:19, DK; Job 28:24, 37:3, 41:11, DK; Dan. 7:27, 9:12, DK

41 Rev. 13:7, NL

42 Rev. 6:9–11, DK

43 Dan. 7:25, 12:7, DK; Rev. 11:2–3, 12:6, 12:9, 12:13–14, 13:5, DK

44 Rev. 6:17, 15:1, 15:7, DK

45 Rev. 12:12, DK

46 1 Thess. 5:9, DK

47 Rev. 6:12–17, DK; Rev. 15:1, DK

48 1 Thess. 4:13–18, DK

49 Dake Bible, NT page 227, col. 2 "Rapture and Second Advent"

50 Gen. 5:24, DK; 2 Kings. 2:11, DK; Luke 23:50– 24:17, DK; Eph. 4:8–10, DK; Heb. 2:14–15, DK; 1 Thess. 4:13–18, DK; Rev. 12:5, DK; Rev. 11:12, DK; Rev. 20:4, DK

51 Dan. 9:27, DK; Matt. 24:15, DK; Mark 13:13–14, DK

52 Luke 21:20, DK

53 Matt. 24:14, DK

54 Zech. 14:1, DK; Joel 2:31, DK; Acts 2:20, DK; 2 Pet. 3:10, DK; Zeph. 1:18, DK; 2 Pet. 3:7, DK

55 Matt. 24:30, DK; Rev. 19:11–21, DK

56 2 Thess. 2:7, DK

57 Rev. 7:2–4, DK; Matt. 24:16–20, DK; Rev. 12:6, 12:14, 12:16, DK

58 Rev. 9:15, DK

59 Dake Bible, OT page 576, col. 1 "Sela or Petra"

60 Matt. 24:22, DK; Mark 13:19–20, DK

61 Zech. 13:8, DK; Dake Bible, OT page 877, col. 3 note 14

62 Dan. 12:1, DK; Dake Bible, NT page 311, col. 4 note 28

63 Dake Bible, OT page 880, col. 2 "The Purpose of Tribulation"

64 Matt. 24:24, NL

65 Rev. 11:3–7, DK

66 Dan. 11:36–39, DK; 2 Thess. 2:3–4, DK; Rev. 13:16–17, 14:9–11, DK

67 Rev. 16:2–4, 16:8–11, DK

68 Dan. 8:14, NL

69 Rev. 11:2, DK

70 Dake Bible, note to 2 Thess. 2:3

71 Acts 2: 17–21, DK; Rev. 4:4, DK

72 Dan. 11:44, 19:19, DK

73 Rev. 16:12, 19:20–21, DK

74 Rev. 16:17–21, DK

75 Dake Bible, OT page 875, col. 1 note 1

76 Dake Bible, NT page 311, col. 3 note 10, col. 4 note 5, col. 4 note 29

Abbreviations

DK Dake Bible, Dake Publishing, Lawrenceville, GA
NL New Living Study Bible, Tyndale House Publishers, Wheaton, IL
NT New Testament
OT Old Testament

Notes, Chapter 14 (continued)

77 Rev. 11:7, DK; Zech. 14:16,
    Dake Bible, NT page 313
    col. 4 "Two Classes of Eter-
    nal People"
78 Rev. 19:7–9, 18–19, DK
79 Zech. 14:1–5, DK; Rev.
    19:19–21, DK
80 Rev. 19:20, 20:3, DK
81 Matt. 25:31–46, DK
82 Dake Bible, NT page 313,
    col. 1 "Restitution of All
    Things"; Dake Bible, OT
    page 882, col. 4 notes 12–13
83 Zech. 14:16, DK; Dake
    Bible, OT page 313, col. 4
    "Two Classes of Eternal
    People"
84 Rev. 20:8, DK
85 Ezek. 48:1–35, DK
86 Rev. 14:9–11, DK

Abbreviations

DK   Dake Bible, Dake Publishing, Lawrenceville, GA
NL   New Living Study Bible, Tyndale House Publishers,
      Wheaton, IL
NT   New Testament
OT   Old Testament

Chapter 15

Eternity

E VIL WILL STILL BE ALIVE on earth during the thousand years following Armageddon – apparently a lot of evil.[1] This evil will endure for some in spite of the fact that they are now experiencing long and peaceable life under the Messiah. As in the days of the exodus, many will still refuse to acknowledge God, even after witnessing all of these events. In keeping with His pattern, God will not force people to follow Him.

At the end of the thousand years, Satan will be released for a brief period (perhaps several years) to collect those remaining in evil throughout the earth. Under Satan's leadership, these people will again gather their evil army around Jerusalem, the headquarters of the Messiah, and God Himself will destroy them all with fire from Heaven before a battle even starts.[2]

Satan will finally be permanently consigned to the lake of fire with the Antichrist and the False Prophet to be tormented day and night forever, as will all others who have failed to take the opportunity for atonement offered by the Messiah's blood.[3]

There will be the Great White Throne judgement. This one-time-only judgement is for the wicked dead. At this event the book of life-history will be opened for each individual who has not willingly submitted to God and accepted sin atonement by the only means He has provided. No one subject to this judgement will get another chance to get to Heaven. All will be permanently consigned to the lake of fire.[4] All of those who have accepted sin atonement will already be in Heaven with God, their sins "blotted out" of their books of life.

Then God will renovate the earth, this time with fire.[5] Seas will be eliminated. The nature of animals will change as those who have been meat-eaters will become vegetarians.[6] All evil will be gone forever after these actions. Somehow, the good natural persons who are committed to God will survive the fire to repopulate the earth, which after this point will produce only good people.[7]

When all evil is removed permanently from earth, God will then move His holy city, Jerusalem, down from Heaven. The city will be about fifteen hundred miles square, and will range up to fifteen hundred miles in height at its peak. He Himself will also move to earth.[8]

The glory of the Lord God and the Messiah will light the new city of Jerusalem, leaving no need for the sun and the moon in that area.[9] There will be no night there.

The "River of Life" will flow throughout the city from the throne of God and the Messiah.[10] And the Messiah and His believers will reign forever and ever. Eternity will have commenced.

Chart 10

A.D. 3000

FUTURE ETERNITY

MILLENNIUM (cont.)

Satan loosed
Evil gathered
Great White Throne judgement
Satan consigned permanently to lake of fire
Renovation by fire
  Seas gone
Holy Jerusalem descends
God moves to earth
Paradise living for natural mankind as in Garden of Eden

Notes, Chapter 15

1   Rev. 20:8, DK
2   Rev. 20:7–9, DK
3   Rev. 20:10, DK
4   Rev. 20:11–15, DK
5   2 Pet. 3:7, 3:10, DK
6   Isa. 11:6–7, 65:25, NL
7   Zech. 14:20, DK; Dake
    Bible, OT page 313, col. 4
    "Two Classes of Eternal
    People"
8   Rev. 21:2–3, 21:16, DK
9   Rev. 21:23, DK
10 Rev. 22:1, NL

Abbreviations

DK   Dake Bible, Dake Publishing, Lawrenceville, GA
NL   New Living Study Bible, Tyndale House Publishers,
     Wheaton, IL
NT   New Testament
OT   Old Testament

Selected Bibliography

Alighieri, Dante. *The Divine Comedy.* New York, NY, Bantam Penguin, 1980.

Anderson, Neil T. *The Bondage Breaker.* Eugene, OR, Harvest House, 1993.

Beirle, Donald. *Surprised by Faith.* Lynnwood, WA, Emerald Books, 1992.

Billheimer, Paul E. *Destined for the Throne.* Minneapolis, MN, Bethany House, 1997.

Billheimer, Paul E. *Don't Waste Your Sorrows.* Minneapolis, MN, Bethany House, 1977.

Dake, Finis. *Dake Bible.* Lawrenceville, GA, Dake Bible Publishing, 1963.

Harley, Willard F. Jr. *His Needs Her Needs.* Grand Rapids, MI, Fleming H. Revell, 1984.

Johnson, Paul, A. *History of the Jews.* New York, NY, Harper Perennial, 1987.

Johnson, Phillip E. *Defeating Darwinism.* Downers Grove, IL, InterVarsity Press, 1997.

Latourette, Kenneth Scott. *A History of Christianity, Vol. 1 & 2.* San Francisco, CA, Harpers, 1975.

Lea, Larry. *Could You Not Tarry One Hour.* Rockwall, TX, Larry Lea Ministries, 1988.

Michener, James. *The Source.* New York, NY, Fawcett Books, 1965.

Moody, Raymond. *Life after Life.* New York, NY, Bantam Books, 1975.

Rosen, Ruth. *Testimonies.* San Francisco, CA, Purple Pomegranate Productions, 1992.

Rosenthal, Marvin. *The Pre-Wrath Rapture of the Church.* Nashville, TN, Thomas Nelson, 1990.

Sachar, Howard M. *A History of Israel from the Rise of Zionism to Our Time.* New York, NY, Alfred A. Knopf, 1996.

Stanley, Charles. *The Blessings of Brokenness.* Grand Rapids, MI, Zondervan, 1997.

Telchin, Stan. *Abandoned.* Grand Rapids, MI, Chosen Books, 1997

Thigpen, Thomas. *Gehenna.* Lake Mary, FL, Creation House, 1992.

VanKampen, Robert. *The Sign,* Wheaton, IL, Crossway Books, 1992.

Walvoord, John. *Every Prophecy of the Bible.* Colorado Springs, CO, Chariot Victor Publishing, 1990.

Index

Money. *See* Materialism
Morality, 22
Moses, 103–104, 107, 109
Muslim. *See* Islam

N

Nebuchadnezzar, 112
New Covenant, 119
Nimrod, 97–98
Noah, 94, 95, 97–100

O

Occult, 19, 55
Offerings. *See* Giving
Old Testament. *See* Bible
Ottoman Empire, 125
Overcoming, 74

P

Pain, 18
Patriarchs, rulers, 103–109
Paul, 51
Peace, 25, 81
Petra, 151–152
Pharisees, 17
Predestination, 55–56
Pride, 24
Prophecies, 112, 126, 133, 135–136
Puzzle design, 30, 31
Pyramid construction, 97, 100

R

Rabbis, 104
Rage, 19
Raptures, 147–149, 156
Rationalism, 32
Reformation, 125
Relationships, 13

Religions, validating, 112–113
Repentance, 51, 70, 74
Resurrection, 17–18
Reverse engineering, 98
River of Life, 166
Roman Catholic church, 120
Roman period, 122

S

Sabbath, 57
Sadducees, 17
Satan
    and behavior, 15, 42, 52
    defeat of, 154, 165
    on earth, 89–90
    flood of, 32, 84, 91
    and God, 83, 105
    purpose, 116
    rights to test, 105–106
    trickery of, 44
    and world system, 25
    wrath of, 151–152
Saul, 108, 109
Scripture. *See* Bible
Seals, 143–145. *See also* Sixth Seal
Second Coming. *See* Dual
    Coming of Messiah
Security, 81. *See also* Eternal
    security
Sela. *See* Petra
Semiramis, 97–98
Seven-year peace pact, 149–141
Seventieth Week, 133, 136–137, 139,
    142–143, 145, 152, 157, 160
Sex and sexuality, 19, 72–73
Sin(s)
    defined, 23
    forgiveness for, 18, 69
    repenting, 51, 70, 74
    See also Good and evil

QUICK ORDER FORM

Telephone Orders: 763-559-3900
Web Orders: mainstreetentertainment.com
Fax Orders: 763-383-0081
Mail Orders: YES! Entertainment, 12866 Highway 55, Minneapolis, MN 55441
For further information, please call 763-559-3900.

ORDER FORM

Please send ____ copies of DON'T LOSE YOUR DESTINY. Cost is $9.95 plus shipping for one copy. For multiple copies, see discount and shipping information below. I may return any of them for any reason, at any time, no questions asked, as long as they are returned in the same condition as new books coming off the press.

NAME

ADDRESS

APT. OR SUITE #

CITY   STATE   ZIP

TELEPHONE

EMAIL ADDRESS

Shipping

☐ US mail: $4 for the first book and $2 for each additional
☐ Next day delivery: $12 for the first book and $2 for each additional
☐ Second day delivery: $9 for the first book and $2 for each additional
☐ International: $9 for first book and $5 for each additional

Minnesota residents please add 6.5% sales tax.

Payment

☐ Check   ☐ Visa   ☐ MasterCard   ☐ Money Order

CARD NUMBER   EXP. DATE

NAME ON CARD

SIGNATURE

Discount Policy

2–4 copies: $7.95 each; 5–9 copies: $6.95 each; 10–24 copies: $5.95 each; 25–49 copies: $5.77 each; 50–74 copies: $5.57 each; 75–99 copies: $5.37 each; 100–199 copies: $5.17 each; 200–499 copies: $4.97 each; 500+ copies: $4.47 each.

About the Author

JIM MCCLEARY was the owner of AmeriData, a 450-employee company that in 1993 began the process of profitably acquiring more than thirty competitors over approximately the same number of months to become a two billion dollar, 3,500-employee, worldwide computer-systems integrator. AmeriData was sold to General Electric in 1996. Jim flunked retirement after a couple of years and has now started two new companies, Main-Street Entertainment, which provides traditional-values family entertainment products, and LogiSolve, an e-business consulting firm. Jim, the father of five, resides in the Midwest.